501
WRITERS'
QUESTIONS
ANSWERED

Nancy Smith

PIATKUS

DEDICATION
For Jane – fellow writer, colleague and friend

Copyright © 1996 by Nancy Smith

First published in Great Britain in 1996 by
Judy Piatkus (Publishers) Ltd of
5 Windmill Street, London W1P 1HF

**The moral right of the author
has been asserted**

*A catalogue record for this book is available
from the British Library*

ISBN 0-7499-1497-1 (hbk)
ISBN 0-7499-1512-9 (pbk)

Edited by Helen Simpson
Designed by Sue Ryall

Set in 10.5/13pt New Baskerville by
Action Typesetting Limited, Gloucester
Printed and bound in Great Britain by
Butler & Tanner Ltd, Frome, Somerset

Contents

Write at the Start

A few years ago, I was privileged to be part of the editorial team at the inception of *Writers News*, the brainchild of David Thomas, owner of the erstwhile Devon publishing house, David & Charles. Having been a teacher of creative writing for many years, I knew of the large number of questions which writers at all points in their career continually ask.

Many of these are of a practical nature: how to find a literary agent; how to submit work correctly to a publisher or editor; how to protect one's copyright. Others concentrate on aspects of technique such as the oft-confusing viewpoint, how and when to use flashback, how to structure and plot a short story. Others come from aspiring writers seeking reassurance about the possibility of success, of whether, indeed, writing is a subject which can be learned.

As commissioning editor of *Writers News*, I initiated and produced the magazine's Helpline which proved to be one of its most popular features. It was Helpline's success that eventually gave birth to the idea of a simple-format question-and-answer book.

There are many books available on the craft of writing, and they deal with a wide range of topics. None, however, seemed to offer a means of quick and easy reference which could be readily accessible on desk or writing table. This is what *501 Writers' Questions Answered* is intended to be.

It is a handy, simple-to-use reference book, which will provide the answers to all the questions you are ever likely to ask, whether you are a complete beginner or already well on the road to success. I hope you will find within its pages everything you wish to know about the fascinating and absorbing subject of writing.

First Steps in Becoming a Writer

Most people, when they first think about becoming a writer, are immediately beset with doubts. Perhaps they are not well-enough educated, haven't enough to write about which will be of interest to others. They wonder, too, if it is possible to learn *how* to write successfully. Indeed, they question whether writing is a subject which can be taught at all. Perhaps writers are born, not made. But, if writing is a craft which can be learned, what is the best way to go about it? And then there is the question of equipment: how much is it necessary to buy and how much will it cost?

All these concerns are normal and natural and need to be addressed right at the start, before even putting pen to paper. Section One does just this, setting out to reassure anyone seriously interested in becoming a writer.

Q.   *How do I know if I have enough talent to make it as a writer?*

A.   Until you actually try putting pen to paper, you'll never find out. Obviously, in order to succeed in this highly competitive field, you need natural, even if latent, talent, a flair for using words correctly and interestingly. For instance, it may be that you like writing letters, and their recipients tell you how much they enjoy them and say, 'You ought to write a book'. Or

3

perhaps English was your favourite or best subject at school, particularly those lessons where you could draw on your imagination to create stories – what was sometimes called 'English composition'. Both these are good indicators of a potential writer. But writing is a craft and, like any other, has to be learned and honed to achieve the expertise necessary for success.

Q. *I've recently retired and I would like to take up writing. But am I too old now, do you think, to have much chance of success?*

A. Fortunately, writing is an occupation you can take up at any age and have as good a chance of success as someone many years younger. Indeed, the fact that you have had so much experience of life will stand you in good stead. The celebrated novelist Pearl Buck once said that no one should attempt to write a novel before they were forty (in other words, before they had *lived*).

In recent years, there have been several instances of authors in their sixties, seventies and even eighties having their first novels published, some of which became bestsellers. Mary Wesley was seventy when she achieved immediate success, and has just published her ninth book. Sybil Marshall is eighty-one and Joyce Windsor's first novel was promoted by W. H. Smith under their Fresh Talent scheme. Joan Brady was in her fifties when she won the prestigious 1993 Whitbread Book of the Year Award for *Theory of War*, her story of a white boy sold into slavery in post-Civil War America, and another American writer, E. Annie Proulx, won a Pulitzer Prize when in her late fifties, with *The Shipping News*.

Literary journalist Judith Rice, writing on the subject, said, 'If you are fifty – better still, eighty – pick up your pen and write. That is the age for literary stardom, now; especially if you are a woman.'

So, if you want to write, begin as you would if it were any other type of craft. Set about learning the necessary techniques, practise, practise, practise and, provided you persevere, success will surely come.

Lastly, remember that, unless your age is relevant to marketing and selling your work, there is no need for any editor or publisher to be made aware of it. You could be eighteen or eighty and no one need know.

Q. *How would you define a professional writer?*

A. First of all, it does not necessarily mean earning your living from writing but it does mean being paid for what you write. This is often a debating point among would-be writers, some of whom argue that being paid doesn't matter so long as your work appears in print. But unless it is on a voluntary basis for, say, your local church or charity magazine, you should treat your writing on a par with any other form of work. Remember the saying that the labourer is worthy of his hire and place a value on yourself and what you do.

It is a question of attitude and you must adopt a professional one if you hope to succeed. This includes presenting and submitting your work correctly so that an editor or publisher knows you are taking it seriously. It means not saying (or thinking), 'This is rubbish,' or 'This isn't any good.' If you think this is true, then you should rethink and rewrite until you honestly believe your piece is as good as you can make it. After all, if *you* think so lowly of it, why should anyone else think differently?

Being a professional means taking infinite care over basic things like grammar and spelling. It also involves commitment. If you agree to produce a piece by a specific time, you must meet your deadline or you may never again be invited to contribute to that particular publication.

It also means being prepared to rewrite if asked and accepting necessary editorial changes in your work without feeling aggrieved.

Q. *Are there any particular attributes one needs to become a writer?*

A. Apart from an overwhelming desire to *write* (as opposed to merely wishing to become a writer), you need to have an inbuilt curiosity about life in general. You must be willing to research painstakingly and to keep what many would consider unsocial hours; and you must insist that family and friends take your efforts seriously and give you sufficient time and space to write.

Finally, you will need to have the courage to continue despite setbacks, to persist in the face of any number of rejections and to believe in yourself even if no one else appears to do so. It seems almost impossible to believe, now, but one of our best-loved novelists, Catherine Cookson, had one of her early efforts rejected with the words 'Strongly advise author not to take up writing as a career' scrawled across the back page in red ink. Fortunately, she refused to take that advice, telling herself that she *would* succeed and went on to do so.

Q. *I've been writing for almost a year with not even a glimmer of success. How can I find out if I'm wasting my time and energy because I've no real talent?*

A. First of all, ask yourself *why* you want to write. Is it because you think it is a glamorous kind of occupation, because you want to be a writer rather than that you want to write (there is a big difference)? If the answer is 'yes', then you are unlikely to succeed because you haven't realised that writing is hard work and is a craft which needs to be learned.

Secondly, remember that a year is a short time in which to master your craft, so keep on practising without worrying too much about selling your work. That will come, eventually, if you don't give up.

Q. *Having been writing for some considerable time, so far without seeing any of my work in print, I've come to the conclusion that it's because I don't know any editors or publishers personally. Would it help if I tried to cultivate such personal contacts?*

A. The only possible advantage in knowing an editor or publisher in a personal capacity is that it might ensure your work had a fair reading. After that, it would stand or fall on its merits. But few successful writers started out with that small advantage and, like most others, launched their careers the hard way: by persevering and by being determined to achieve success, however long it took. It is a myth that, to sell your work, you need to know someone in the magazine or book world.

Q. *I'm a total beginner at this writing game and I don't know if I'm being too ambitious in trying to write fiction. Would I be better off having a go at articles?*

A. There is little doubt that articles (that is, non-fiction) are easier to write – and sell – than fiction. Although the short story, obviously, is short and therefore quicker to write than a novel, it is not necessarily easier. Most articles are based on one's own experiences or on thorough research into a particular subject. They too are short and so can be produced relatively quickly. Another advantage is that they can help build up confidence in yourself as a writer as one or two acceptances to your credit will undoubtedly boost your morale.

Q. *I've submitted dozens of articles and short stories to numerous different markets but all I have to show for months of hard work is a collection of rejection slips. None gives any indication as to why my work was rejected. How can I find out the reason?*

A. In part, the answer to this is the same as that to the last question. You need to think carefully about the type of work you are attempting. You would be wise to concentrate, at least for a while, on one or the other, either articles or short stories, wherever your preference lies, rather than on both.

ACQUIRING THE NECESSARY SKILLS

Q. *I'd love to try to write a book but I haven't had much formal education as I left school at fourteen, though I've always been a prolific reader of fiction. How necessary do you think it is to be well-educated, and ought I to take a basic English course first?*

A. Lack of a formal education is no bar to writing success, although you must still use good grammar and correct spelling. These can be learned at any age but, in any case, can be checked once the creative part of your writing is completed and before sending your work out. In fact, it is sometimes said that too formal an education can in itself prove a barrier to creativity. If you have strong feelings on any subject, let them pour out on to the paper without worrying about grammar. If you have a good story to tell, write it first and then check your spelling and so on, afterwards, either with a dictionary or grammar book or by getting someone whose English you trust to read it through and make any necessary corrections.

There are many writers who became best-selling novelists despite a lack of education, so never let this stop you from trying.

Q. *Are there any rules for writing which, once learned, would assure one of success?*

A. Somerset Maugham once said, wryly, 'There are three

rules for writing. Unfortunately, no one can remember what they are.'

Think of the word 'rules' as being in inverted commas, perhaps, or merely as guidelines. But remember, just as the painter needs to understand perspective and the musician harmony, the writer must understand how to use words (which are his only tools) *effectively*. Thus, there are certain do's and don'ts with regard to style and structure which it is wise to learn and stick to (and which will be covered in the appropriate sections in this book).

Having said that, there are no guarantees of success. All anyone can do is learn as much as possible about his craft, then practise and persevere and hope that, in time, success will come. But it is more likely to arrive if you understand and abide by those 'rules' of style and technique which have stood the test of time.

Q. *I don't want to waste my time if I can't be sure of getting my writing published. Are there any short cuts?*

A. In a word, No. Writing is hard work, the operative word being 'work'. You need to spend time studying and analysing your chosen market, making sure your material – fiction or non-fiction – is right for it. Then write and rewrite until it is as polished as you can possibly make it, however long this takes. Only then should you submit it, correctly presented. There is no short cut to this sequence if you hope to be successful.

Writing Classes

Q. *I've just started writing and have been advised to join a class run by my local education authority, but I'm not at all sure that writing is a subject which can be taught. Do you think it can?*

A. To a large extent, writing is a craft and, like any other, there are elements which can be taught. Also, as in all the arts – painting, music, drama and so on – there are techniques which you need to understand and master in order to become proficient. From this point of view, therefore, you should find it definitely helpful if an experienced and successful writer at least sets you on the right path and helps prevent you from making certain elementary mistakes.

All writers must learn their craft in one way or another. Some do so through the prolific reading, and unconscious analysis, of works of published authors. Indeed, Somerset Maugham once said that the best way to learn about novel-writing was to study the craftsmanship of successful novelists. Others, however, prefer to seek instruction in some form or other. At the start of his long and successful career, John Steinbeck, one of the giants of modern literature, was prepared to sit in a creative writing class and be taught.

Creative writing has long been on the syllabuses of many universities in the United States and for some considerable time has been available at various universities in the UK. As a result, several notable novelists have emerged.

Writers' Circles

Q. *Would joining a writers' circle be of benefit now that I've just taken up writing?*

A. Belonging to a writing group of any kind, whether it be a class with a teacher or a circle of writers with varying degrees of expertise and success, undoubtedly brings benefit from personal contact and resultant mutual stimulus and encouragement. It should also provide objective feedback on members' work when read out to the group. However, make sure the group is one which has a professional attitude, which offers honest, constructive criticism of work and, if possible, has among its members some successful writers. A cosy, self-congratulatory group is of no help at all.

Q. *I've recently joined a writers' circle where we read out our work. The trouble is that I find I frequently get conflicting criticism and advice. How much attention should I pay to it?*

A. Listen to all of it, digest it at your leisure, then make up your own mind and discard anything which, *objectively*, you disagree with. Never dismiss the comments of others out of hand, though, as someone else can often spot what is wrong with a particular piece. That is one of the advantages of belonging to a good writers' circle.

Q. *I understand the need to look at one's writing objectively but I find it extremely difficult. Have you any suggestions about how to do this?*

A. It is not easy to be entirely objective about one's own work, which is why it can be advantageous to belong to a writers' circle. If that is impossible, put your work away for at least three weeks, and preferably longer, then reread it in as detached a way as possible. Invariably, you will see where it might be improved, the style tightened, perhaps some cuts made, a word or phrase changed here and there. By doing this, you should improve your chances of acceptance.

Q. *I'd like to join a writers' circle but how do I find out if there is one and where it is held?*

A. There is a useful *Directory of Writers' Circles* (see Useful Publications), which lists most of them around the country. *Writers News* also includes a list, annually, and your public library ought to be able to give you details of any local circle.

Correspondence Courses

Q. *Would I find it useful to take one of the correspondence courses for writers that are often advertised?*

A. This is very much an individual choice. If you want to work at your own pace and in the privacy of your own home, then a correspondence course could prove right for you though, obviously, some courses will be better than others.

Q. *How do correspondence school courses operate?*

A. Normally, you will be set an assignment which, when completed, you return either direct to your tutor or to the school's office. It will be commented upon and returned to you along with the next assignment. In this way, you should be able to make progress in a logical sequence and without any pressure to finish a piece of work within a particular time. One big advantage is that being set a specific task helps you get down to doing some writing.

Q. *I'm thinking of taking a correspondence course in writing. How can I find out which would be the best one and if it is reputable?*

A. First of all, make sure it is run by a bona fide and well-established organisation such as *Writers News, Freelance Press Services* or *Freelance Writing and Photography*. Alternatively, it should be recognised by either the Council for the Accreditation of Correspondence Colleges (CACC) or the Association of British Correspondence Colleges (ABCC), both of which should ensure a certain standard of teaching. Then try to talk to someone who has taken the one you are considering to see if they are satisfied with it.

Q. *I'm considering taking a correspondence course and one offers a money-back guarantee if, at the end of it, I haven't earned* *my fee through my writing. How genuine is such an offer and is there a catch?*

A.   Provided the correspondence course in question belongs to one of the two umbrella bodies mentioned previously, the money-back guarantee should be genuine. The catch lies in the fact that a large number of students give up without completing the course, in which case, of course, they cannot expect to have their money returned. However, provided you have sufficient determination and staying power to work your way through it to the end and if you have not earned your fee by then, there should be no problem in obtaining a refund of the money you have paid out. You will naturally be expected to prove that you have submitted work for publication and have had it rejected.

Other Methods of Learning

Books about Writing

Q.   *There seem to be a great many books available about writing. How useful are they and how should I choose which to buy?*

A.   Many such books specialise in specific areas such as novel-writing, short stories, articles and so on, so choose one or more which cover your own particular area of interest. But you may also find one with a more general focus would be useful, too. The Writers Book Society's book club for writers (run by Writers News Ltd) includes a wide selection of titles.

Q.   *As I already have several books on the craft or writing, is there any point in buying new ones when they appear?*

A.   Because writing is a craft and, as with all crafts, there is always something else to learn about it, new books on the subject will often throw a fresh light on a particular aspect or cover a new or unusual angle. The only danger is that you spend too long reading instead of actually writing.

Writing Magazines

Q.   *Is there anything to be gained from subscribing to a writing magazine?*

A.   Yes, regardless of the point you are at in your writing career. Most will carry features on various aspects of the craft but will also help you keep up to date with market requirements and provide other essential information such as details of competitions and forthcoming literary events. *Writers News*, exclusive to members, is the largest of these. Its sister magazine, *Writing Magazine*, is available on the news-stand (see Useful Publications, p. 199).

Writing Conferences

Q.   *Is there any advantage in attending writers' conferences and seminars? As they are quite expensive, I wonder if they're worth the cost?*

A.   Most such events will include on their programme lectures on various connected topics given either by successful writers or, often, by publishers, editors or literary agents. But they also enable writers to get together to discuss problems, markets and, generally, keep each other up to date with what is happening in the field.

Writing is a lonely business and the stimulus and encouragement gained from others in the same situation can be of immense help. Thus, if you can afford to attend even one of these functions per year, you would probably find it beneficial. Remember, too, that their cost can usually be offset against income tax.

Q.   *I'd like to combine a holiday, or even a weekend break, with* *learning a bit more about writing. Is there any source of information about where courses are held?*

A. There is a useful booklet called *Time to Learn*, which lists most such courses. It is available from NIACE, 19b De Montfort Street, Leicester LE1 7GE, and costs about £5.

Competitions

Q. *I've very recently taken up writing and have just subscribed to a writing magazine which regularly runs a short story competition. Would it be helpful if I began entering such competitions?*

A. Yes indeed. Entering competitions is an excellent way of training yourself to meet deadlines and some also offer a critique which can be invaluable. *Writers News* regularly lists the full range of current competitions, including those run by the David Thomas Charitable Trust. *Quartos* also has a regular competition news feature and runs its own in-house competitions.

Critique Services

Q. *As a fairly new writer, I haven't much confidence in my writing and find it hard to view it objectively. Would it help to use a professional criticism service?*

A. Sometimes it can, because it is always difficult to judge one's own work. However, it can be expensive to use such a service so it might be advisable to continue writing for practice without submitting it to an editor or publisher until you feel more confident. Once you believe you have begun to master your craft and think you are ready to start sending work out, then might be the time to pay for professional criticism.

EQUIPMENT

Typewriter, Wordprocessor or PC

Q. *I've just taken up writing, and hope to make it a part-time career, eventually. I can't afford to spend much money on purchasing equipment but do I need to buy a personal computer or even a typewriter, right away?*

A. You must submit typed work, whether you do it yourself or pay someone to do it for you. If the latter, it will prove far more costly in the long run than if you were to buy yourself a machine of some kind and produce your own typescripts. (Although the term 'manuscript' is still generally used, nowadays, it is a misnomer and 'typescript' is more accurate.) If you have to cut down on initial expenditure, you can buy second-hand electronic typewriters relatively cheaply. However, remember that work produced on a wordprocessor or a personal computer with wordprocessing software (PC) looks much more professional and is also easier to correct. Again, you may be able to buy a second-hand wordprocessor or PC at considerably less cost than a new one, though bear in mind that it will not be covered by a guarantee should it go wrong soon afterwards. A PC's average life-span is about five or six years, depending on how much it is used, so you would be unlucky to have problems if it is only a year or two old. Whatever you buy, take time to look at all the different options before purchasing and discuss the pros and cons of each choice not only with salespeople but with other writers. Once you have bought your machine or system, you will want to keep it for some time.

Q. *Would I find it difficult to change over from an ordinary type-writer to a PC? I am rather daunted by modern technology!*

A. Initially, you might find it difficult or strange if you are not computer-literate and have never used a PC before. It's probably a good idea to take a short course on using one (many local authorities run such classes). Be prepared for it to take a little while to become accustomed to it – but, once you are, you will wonder how you ever managed without it. Revision of work is so much quicker and easier with a PC, eliminating hours of typing, and some book publishers will look more favourably on work produced on a PC.

Using a Wordprocessor/PC

Q. *I want to buy either a wordprocessor or a PC but am bewildered by the number of different machines on the market. Have you any advice to offer?*

A. It is important to consider carefully, before making what will be quite a major purchase, exactly what you want it to do for you. Wordprocessors are a sort of sophisticated typewriter and may therefore seem less daunting in some respects. Their main advantages are portability and price – they are significantly cheaper than the cheapest laptop computer. However, many of them do not have a great deal of built-in memory and they may not be compatible with publishers' software systems: as more and more editing is done on-screen rather than on the printed typescript, this is a point worth bearing in mind.

If you decide to opt for a PC (which may be a more sensible decision in the long-term), you have two main choices: an Apple Mac or an IBM-compatible. If you choose the latter, you will then have to decide what sort of software you want to use. There is a wide range: for those who aren't computer-literate, software that makes much use of a mouse, such as some of the those used with Windows, may be the easiest way in. For the more experienced, a keyboard-orientated package such as WordPerfect may be quicker to use and therefore preferable. Freelances and writers who want to submit material on disk or through e-mail (a fast-growing trend) need to take advice on which software packages are most widely used in the publications of their target markets, and ensure that their own software is, or can be converted to be, compatible. You will, of course, also need to buy a printer to go with your PC.

Printers

Q.   *What sort of printer should I buy?*

A.   It's advisable to buy the best you can afford, even if you don't want to use all its facilities (such as, say, colour printing) right away. It will usually save money in the long run, because there'll be no need to upgrade for a long time.

Dot-matrix printers were once of fairly poor quality, but today editors and publishers will happily look at work printed on a dot-matrix printer *provided* that you use well-inked ribbons, ensuring that your work can be easily read and photocopied. These ribbons are cheap to buy and can be re-inked. Dot-matrix printers print more quickly and quietly than a daisy-wheel.

The more sophisticated – though fairly expensive – laser printers and the excellent and much cheaper ink-jet printers now available are far superior in finish. However, the cost of replacement components, such as the replacement toner cartridges for laser printers, can be alarmingly expensive.

Other Equipment

Q.   *Is there any other equipment I should buy? I need to keep outlay to a minimum.*

A.   A desk or table is a 'must', of course, and a proper typist's chair to support your back is advisable. Access to a telephone, a few good reference books (see Writer's Bookshelf, p. 20), a plentiful supply of paper, a filing cabinet or, at least, some system for filing material is probably all you need to begin with.

Q. *What kind of paper should I buy? Does it have to be the most expensive?*

A. Top-quality paper obviously looks better than a cheaper kind but it invariably costs more and is heavier and so postage also costs more. Instead, use either medium-weight bond paper (100 gsm) or good-quality photocopying paper – but *never* 'flimsy' or bank paper. It is always cheaper to buy a ream (500 sheets) at a time. You might also consider joining forces with several other writers, perhaps a group who belong to the same writers' circle, to buy in bulk.

Q. *Can you suggest a simple and cheap method of filing potentially useful newspaper clippings, etc?*

A. Old, large envelopes, clearly labelled, is the cheapest method if you don't want to invest in a more elaborate filing system or filing cabinet.

Q. *Is it necessary or advisable to buy a fax machine?*

A. A fax machine is not essential unless you intend regularly submitting a fair number of non-fiction features. You might, though, find one useful at times, especially if speed is of the essence in getting a particular piece to an editor.

Q. *Is there any other equipment I should consider buying?*

A. You might find it worth investing in a simple, inexpensive answer-phone, giving out a message to callers that you will be available to speak to them between specific hours. That should undoubtedly minimise distractions and save you precious writing time. The disadvantage is that your telephone bill might increase as you return calls, but you can overcome that problem by including in your message a request that the caller phones again at certain times. It is possible to buy, now, at fairly reasonable prices, machines which combine telephone, answer-phone and fax, which might prove of considerable benefit.

Q. *Having started out as a writer, I want to create a good impression when I submit work for publication. Ought I to have letter-headed paper printed and perhaps business cards?*

A. It is not necessary at this point but, if you can afford it, it would help create a professional image to have some letter-head paper printed.

Q. *I've been selling articles on a fairly regular basis and now want to branch out by using my own illustrations. I'm not an expert photographer, so what sort of camera should I buy?*

A. A good-quality, automatic camera should be adequate. Choose one made by a reputable firm such as Canon, Olympus, Nikon, Pentax or Minolta. Later on, if you find you have an aptitude for photography and are prepared to invest in better equipment, you might consider upgrading to a single-lens reflex model. In the meantime, though, an automatic should produce results good enough for reproduction in magazines.

Writer's Bookshelf

Q. *Are there any reference books which I ought to buy at the start of my career as a writer?*

A. It is useful for any writer to have to hand a comprehensive and up-to-date dictionary, a thesaurus and a grammar book such as *A Dictionary of Modern English*

Usage by H. W. Fowler or *The Oxford Guide to English Usage*. Also, perhaps, *The Oxford Dictionary for Writers and Editors*, a dictionary of quotations such as *The New Penguin Dictionary of Quotations* or *The Oxford Dictionary of Quotations*, *Brewers' Dictionary of Phrase and Fable*, *Research for Writers* by Ann Hoffmann and either *The Writer's Handbook* or *The Writers' and Artists' Year Book*. An encyclopedia might also prove useful, perhaps *Chronicle of the 20th Century* or *Chambers Dictionary of World History* and an up-to-date world atlas. Gradually, you can build up a small library of varying types of works of reference which, over the years, should earn their place on it.

SUMMING UP

Your fears are now allayed. You know that writing is, indeed, a craft and that it is possible to learn the techniques involved. You have also been reassured that lack of a formal education, of itself, is no barrier to success. You have also considered the basic equipment you will need when you begin. You can now move confidently on to the next stage.

Getting Started

Having overcome initial doubts, the next step is to look at how and where to start. Most of us lead busy lives but finding time and space for your writing, somewhere where you can be undisturbed for even a little while, is essential. It is useful to look at some of the ways in which you can organise this. Then there is the need to devise a practicable working method which is suitable for *you*, to look at how to find ideas, if these are temporarily lacking, and to consider some of the basic rules of writing. For instance, what does 'style' mean and how do you set about developing a good one and finding your own voice?

These are essentially practical issues which will help smooth your path at a time when you may lack confidence in your ability as a writer and before you make that first sale, after which you can legitimately say, 'I am a writer'.

SPACE AND TIME TO WRITE

Q. *Because of work and family commitments, I don't get much time to myself but I would like to start writing. How can I make time and space for it?*

A. Finding time and space for yourself is always difficult for someone with a very busy life but it is necessary if you are serious about writing. Even half an hour every day is better than nothing. Could you get up an hour earlier each morning to give yourself a brief, undisturbed period? Could you re-organise your life to allow yourself a couple of hours . every week, perhaps? Producing even a few hundred words every week would go a long way to completing a novel in a year.

It's mostly a question of determination and making sure that those around you realise how important wrting is to you. Make them take it as seriously as you do and ask them to co-operate in freeing up a little time each week for you. As regards physical space, a quiet corner with a notepad and pen is all that is absolutely necessary. Many successful writers complete the creative part this way, before getting down to typing it up.

Q. *Is it a good idea to write at a regular time each day?*

A. It is undoubtedly advisable, if at all possible. The mind is rather like a clock which is wound up regularly and slips into writing mode more readily if it is trained to work at a particular hour each day.

WHERE TO START

Q. *How soon after taking up writing should I start sending work out in the hope of publication?*

A. That will depend upon the type of writing you do, your own natural talent and the amount of work you put into it. If you begin with articles, and either write about what you know or research a particular subject and know which market it is suitable for, there is no reason why you should not submit your work right away. However, if you are trying your hand at fiction (the short story,

for instance), it would be wiser to give yourself sufficient time to learn your craft as, otherwise, you might
become discouraged by rejections and give up before
you've given yourself a chance.

Q. *What are the best types of markets for a beginner to aim at?*

A. Small-circulation publications, such as local newspapers which are not likely to pay much for material
used, church or business newsletter-type magazines
(these almost certainly will not pay at all but are useful
for honing your skills, at the start of your career) and
any specialist magazines dealing with subjects with
which you are familiar.

Local radio is another possible outlet. Again, it is
unlikely to pay more than a few pounds but it is good
practice for writing words that will be spoken rather
than read.

Q. *I accept that I have a lot to learn about writing and am not
worrying about submitting work for ages, yet. How can I
usefully practise my craft at this stage?*

A. Keep a regular journal, noting in it scraps of overheard
dialogue, observations about people you meet during
the day, descriptions of the weather, impressions of
places and events. This will not only provide good
writing practice but should prove useful, later on, if you
decide to branch out into fiction.

Q. *I've sold some six articles and a couple of short stories and
very much want to become a full-time writer. Have I had sufficient success to take the plunge and give up my regular job?*

A. Obviously, this will depend on individual circumstances. Do you have a private income, for instance,
which would support you, initially? Unless you have
some other means of financial support, it would be

unwise to give up regular employment in order to try to make a living from freelance writing which, at the best of times, is precarious. Better by far to continue to write in your spare time until you are making as much from writing as from your normal job. At that point, you would be in a position to re-assess the situation.

Q. *I've always been blessed with a lot of imagination so I wonder if it would be best to start with fiction rather than non-fiction?*

A. Having a good imagination is obviously essential for anyone wishing to write fiction but a good deal more is needed to achieve success in this field. The main advantage of starting with articles for magazines or newspapers is that they are simpler to write and easier to sell because there is a vast market open to the freelance. However, the decision must be yours. If fiction is your sole aim, maybe that is where you should concentrate your talents.

Q. *I've had several letters published in the national press. I'd like to progress from there and not only see my writing in print but also get paid for it. What would, logically, be the next step?*

A. Many magazines have letters pages which invite contributions from readers for which they pay a sum of money or, sometimes, offer a prize. Amounts paid vary from magazine to magazine but not a few writers have started their career with these, earning quite a considerable sum in a year. It is also a good way of learning how to study a particular market because it is just as important to consider length, subject matter and the readership of the magazine when aiming for the letters page as it is when writing a feature article. But a word of warning: never send the same letter to more than one magazine.

Q. *My main aim in starting to write is, unashamedly, to make money. I've heard that romantic novels are among the highest-*

paid forms of writing and they appear so simple that I think they must be extremely easy to write. Although I don't enjoy reading them, I feel sure I could write them. Should I try?

A. There is nothing wrong with hoping to make money from writing: after all, it will have involved a lot of effort and, as Samuel Johnson famously said, 'no man but a blockhead ever wrote except for money'. However, to set out to write in a genre you don't enjoy reading is unlikely to result in success. Tongue-in-cheek romantic fiction will never work. The lack of conviction would quickly become apparent to the readers, who would be unable to suspend their disbelief (though the book would be unlikely to get beyond a publisher's reader). Far better to concentrate your efforts in another field and have money as the result rather than the goal.

Q. *I've been told a good way to get started is by writing fillers? What are they?*

A. A filler is a very short piece, mostly non-fiction, which, as the name suggests, is used to fill in small gaps in editorial magazines. Length varies but is usually between 150 and 350 words. It can be a humorous anecdote, probably based on an everyday experience, a household hint, a pertinent quote – almost anything which would grab a reader's attention for a brief time. As with any other form of writing, you must study the market to find out which takes which kind of material and how much. Nowadays, some magazines include a great many fillers as part of their standard material so it is a useful place to begin your career.

FINDING IDEAS

Q. *Can you suggest a way of coming up with ideas for magazine articles?*

A.   One way is, whenever you read a magazine feature which you enjoy, ask yourself if there is any aspect of it which you found particularly interesting. Then ask if you might be able to concentrate on that one aspect or angle and expand on it. If it had a general or national slant, can you think of a regional one, maybe involving a local personality whom you could interview? Or did it have a regional flavour which could be extended to suit a magazine with a country-wide circulation?

Another method is to brainstorm, making a list of your expertise and life experiences. You may surprise yourself at the amount of knowledge you possess which would interest other people. For instance, someone who had spent their working life in the candle-making industry should be able to produce a popular 'how to' article on making Christmas candles. They might also have enough material, especially if they did some research into the subject, to write one about the history of candles.

Look out for items of interest in the media which suggest possible topics. Suppose you learned that a new perfume had just been discovered, using an unusual flower. Your local reference library would almost certainly have information about the manufacture of perfume, and you could research the history of perfume and its uses down the ages.

Check on forthcoming anniversaries well in advance, both annual ones such as the New Year or St Valentine's Day and those commemorating events of, say, twenty-five, fifty or a hundred years ago. These will usually produce saleable features.

It is a question of keeping your eyes, ears and mind open for subjects which it might be possible to turn into saleable articles.

Ideas for Fiction

Q. *Is there any quick and easy way to find ideas for short stories?*

A. Ideas are all around us. It is developing them that usually presents the difficulty. Short anecdotal items in newspapers can often provide the basis for a story, so clipping out any which interest or intrigue you and keeping them in an ideas file is a useful way of ensuring you have a plentiful supply when you need them. But remember, an idea is not a plot and you need to build on it to produce a workable storyline.

Another method is to take three separate objects – for example, a walking-stick, a letter and a dog – and weave a story around them. Or you could take the opening line of a published story and use it as a springboard to get one of your own started. You would have to rewrite the beginning at some point, of course, so that it was your own and not someone else's. Yet another useful source is the 'agony aunt' columns in newspapers and magazines. Take a reader's problem as the starting point, then build on it to turn it into fiction.

Q. *Sometimes, when I'm out and about, or when I wake during the night, I get a wonderful idea for a story or 'hear' in my head a brilliant line of dialogue. But often, by the time I'm back home or get up, I can't recall it. Have you any suggestions how to deal with this?*

A. No self-respecting writer should ever be without a notebook and pen or pencil to hand. Ideas and observations have a habit of arriving at inconvenient times and, if not recorded immediately, tend to slip away and be lost for ever. Always jot down in your notebook a key word or phrase, which will usually be sufficient to remind you of the whole when you are in a position to write it out fully.

Q. *How important is inspiration in writing?*

A. There is a well-known saying that writing is ten per cent inspiration and ninety per cent perspiration. That about sums it up, though there are times when inspiration seems to be more than usually active so that one's writing flows more easily. But, inspired or not, good writing entails much hard work.

WORKING METHODS

Q. *I find it difficult to sit down at my typewriter at the same time each day and for the same length of time. Is it really necessary to keep strict working hours?*

A. Obviously this will vary from person to person but most professional writers agree that having a regular working schedule is not only beneficial but necessary to maintain output. If you think of your writing as a job with regular hours, it may help you overcome this problem which is often one of self-discipline.

Q. *Sometimes when I'm in the middle of writing, I can't think of the exact word I want. Should I stop and search for it or leave it till later?*

A. Leave a space and continue writing, otherwise, by the time you have found the word you want, you may find you have interrupted the flow and lose far more time getting started once more.

Q. *Can you suggest a suitable and practicable working method?*

A. Each writer must find his/her own but it is a definite help to write at the same time each day, even if only for half an hour. Some find it best to set themselves a target of so many words, say 500, every day, depending on how much time they have available. Some can write only in longhand initially, while others prefer to create directly on to typewriter or PC. The latter method undoubtedly speeds up the entire process but many find it inhibits their creativity and need to produce their first draft, at least, by hand. Experiment until you discover the method which suits you best.

Q. *How many words should I aim to produce each day?*

A. All writers work at different speeds and in different ways. Some cannot move on to the next part of a story until they have perfected the previous one, so will work quite slowly, perhaps producing only a few hundred words each day. Others will write the first draft rapidly, perhaps producing two or three thousand words a day but knowing they will have to do extensive revision later.

    If it helps with the self-discipline, set yourself a realistic target (perhaps 500 or 1000 words a day) and stick to it, not letting yourself leave your desk until you have finished. If you don't manage them on one day, make up the number the following day.

WRITER'S BLOCK

Q. *What is meant by the term 'writer's block'?*

A. Opinions differ as to whether there is actually any such thing but anyone who has experienced it knows only too well how frightening it can be. It mostly affects novelists, leaving them in a state of mind in which they desperately want to be able to write or develop a story but all creativity seems to have dried up. The more they try to force themselves to write, the more they find the ideas won't flow. It is a frightening situation for any writer to find himself in.

Q. *I've been suffering from the dreaded writer's block for more than six months and feel I'll never be able to write again. How can I overcome it?*

A. First of all, try to eliminate any obvious causes such as tiredness, overwork or anxiety about outside problems, any of which can prevent the creative juices flowing. Or it may be a question of attempting to write the wrong story, and putting it aside, at least for a while, would solve the problem. In the meantime, try to find a story-line which excites you, then give it sufficient time to incubate, for you to get to know the characters fully and understand their motivations, before starting work on it. Lastly, consider if your subconscious is telling you your creative well needs time to refill. In this case, forcing yourself to write is likely to do more harm than good and the wisest course might be to relax, read, do some physical work such as gardening or undertake research into any topic which interests you. When the time is right, the urge to put pen to paper will surface again if you truly want to write. One thing is certain: the more you worry about writer's block, the worse it will become.

Q. *I often find it difficult to get started each day. How can I overcome this kind of writer's block?*

A. Many writers find they need some sort of gimmick to get them started each day, and it's a question of finding one that suits you. Perhaps the most useful tip is to finish the last writing stint in the middle of a sentence, paragraph or page, so that when you return to it you are not faced with a blank sheet of paper. You may find it easier to click into gear and pick up the thread of the story where you left off.

RESEARCH

Q. *I need some up-to-the-minute medical information for the novel I'm writing. Would my doctor or medical centre be willing to talk to me, do you think?*

A. Yes – never be afraid to consult the experts. They will usually be happy to talk about their subject to a serious writer. But go about it in a professional manner. Ring or write first, explaining why you would like to speak to someone, and ask for an appointment. Then, before you go, make sure your questions are written down so that you don't waste their time.

Q. *Is there anywhere I can see a copy of a newspaper published at the end of the last century?*

A. The British Library Newspaper Library, Colindale Avenue, London NW9 5HE (tel: 0171-323 7353) will have one as it is the major holding of both national and foreign newspapers and periodicals published since the 1700s. The Library is open Monday to Saturday from 10 a.m. to 4.45 p.m. A reader's pass is needed, available from the Library.

Q. *Is there any advice you could give me in respect of the research I'm undertaking for the novel I'm writing set in sixteenth-century England?*

A. The most important thing is to keep in mind the importance of checking – and double-checking – facts. Also, whenever possible go to primary rather than secondary sources. Primary sources are original documentation, such as letters or diaries, while secondary sources are what someone other than the originator of the material has written about it. A book you might find useful is *Research For Writers* by Ann Hoffmann, published by A. & C. Black. Bibliographies in books on the subject should also offer useful leads to source material.

Q. *I often want to track down a particular quotation. Can you recommend a useful book?*

A. There are various books on the market which contain a large number of well-known quotations, among them *The Oxford Dictionary of Quotations* and *The Penguin Dictionary of Quotations* (both still in print). Another, now out of print but which you might find in a library or second-hand bookshop, is *The Book of Unusual Quotations*, selected by Rudolf Flesch and published by Cassell.

Q. *Apart from public libraries, are there any other places where I might be able to find reference books on a variety of subjects?*

A. Among the best are The British Museum Reading Room and the Bodleian Library at Oxford University, for both of which you need to apply for a reader's ticket. The London Library is a private subscription library (see Useful Addresses, p. 195), invaluable to anyone living outside London as it offers a comprehensive postal service.

Q. *Are there people or agencies who will undertake research on a fee-paying basis? If so, how do I locate them?*

A. Yes. You will find them listed in *The Writers' and Artists' Year Book* and *The Writer's Handbook* under Editorial and Research services. The British Library Reference Division, as well as other libraries, should be able to provide lists of names and addresses on receipt of an SAE.

STYLE

Q. *What exactly is meant by 'style'?*

A. There are various definitions. It has been said that 'style is the man' or, in modern idiom, it is a writer's own, distinctive voice. Jonathan Swift suggested that it is 'proper words in proper places'. It is concerned with the manner in which a piece is written, not with what it says, that is, with form rather than content. Joseph Conrad, in his preface to *The Nigger of the 'Narcissus'*, said: 'My task ... is, by the power of the written word, to make you hear, to make you feel – it is, before all, to make you *see*! That – and no more, and it is everything!'

Q. *What is a journalistic style?*

A. It is crisp and concise with short sentences and paragraphs rather than long. No sentence should have more than about twenty-seven words in it. Short words are normally preferred to long. It will be lively, too, usually being broken up by quotes in dialogue form and with plenty of action verbs. It is precise and not repetitive and should sound natural, not stilted and formal through the pedantic use of correct grammar.

Every word should count and your meaning should be precise. For example, far too often we hear the statement that someone 'hopes to do something as soon as possible'. This is sloppy writing because, clearly, you are stating that you *will* do something as soon as possible. Otherwise, you should say you 'hope to do something soon'.

Q. *Are there any rules of good style?*

A. There are some generally agreed principles which will result in a good writing style. George Orwell suggested six:

    1. Never use a metaphor, simile or other figure of speech which you are used to seeing in print.
    2. Never use a long word where a short one will do.

3. If it's possible to cut out a word, do so.
4. Never use the passive voice when you can use the active. (An active verb is always more forceful. For example: 'The bullet hit him' rather than 'He was hit by the bullet'.)
5. Never use jargon or foreign phrases if you can find an English equivalent.
6. Break any of these rules, if necessary.

Q. *What is meant by 'tight' writing?*

A. This is another way of describing a style in which words are used carefully and sparingly. For instance, the constant repetition of a word or phrase, the use of clichés, unnecessarily repeating a character's name, over-use of speech tags (he said; she replied; he retorted) and so on, all make for a loose style which is the opposite of 'tight'. Cutting and pruning, that is, taking out any 'dead wood', almost always improves any piece of writing.

Q. *I've heard that one should write for the ear and not the eye. What does this mean?*

A. Narrative should have a pleasing rhythm, which can best be achieved by hearing your sentence structures in your head or, even better, by speaking the words out loud. Often, merely cutting out a word or switching it to another position in the sentence will improve that rhythm. The sound of the words used, if carefully chosen, will add to the effect you are aiming to create. The following brief extract from James Joyce's *A Portrait of the Artist as a Young Man* illustrates this:

> There was a long rivulet in the strand and, as he waded slowly up its course, he wondered at the endless drift of seaweed. Emerald and black and russet and olive, it moved beneath the current, swaying and turning.

Joyce's passage perfectly suggests the movement of seaweed beneath the water. But suppose you rewrote this passage, altering the sequence of words on the following lines, would the effect be lessened?

> He waded slowly up a long rivulet in the strand, wondering at the endless drift of seaweed. Emerald, black, russet and olive, it swayed and turned beneath the current.

That conveys the same information but has lost much of the sense of rhythm, part of which was conveyed by the addition of 'and' between the colours and replacing the slower pace of the present participle ('swaying and turning') with the harder sound of the past tense.

Although we may not think in terms of hearing a piece of prose when we are reading, instinctively we actually do just that, which is why writing for the ear is a good maxim to keep in mind.

Q.   *Recently, my novel was returned by a publisher with the comment that the writing was 'pedestrian'. What does that mean?*

A.   It implied that the style was rather dull and ordinary. That was, of course, the opinion of only one editor and another might not agree. However, there might be an element of truth in it, so take a fresh, objective look and see if you can improve it. Perhaps some colourful and original imagery, introducing symbolism, more effective dialogue and so on would increase its attractiveness to the reader.

Q.   *My style has been criticised for being repetitive but many renowned writers use repetition for effect. Why is it wrong for me to do so?*

A.   When a writer repeats a word or phrase deliberately *in order to create a specific effect*, that repetition is used as a tool. However, when it is there by accident, not only is it ineffective but it becomes tedious and demonstrates a careless style.

Q. *What is a cliché?*

A. It is a phrase or expression which has been used so often that it has lost all its freshness. It has been described as being a word or phrase which originally was so popular that it is apt to be used indiscriminately. For example: leave no stone unturned; beyond the pale; legs like jelly; a heart of gold. No self-respecting writer would consider using such phrases.

The word itself is French and meant a printer's stereotype plate which saved time when typesetting.

Q. *I've been told you should never use clichés, but even Shakespeare used them, didn't he, so why shouldn't I?*

A. The point here is that many of what we now call clichés were first used (that is, were invented) by the Great Bard. To continue to employ them in a piece of prose, as if they were as fresh today as they were many years ago, is to label yourself a lazy writer.

The exception is, of course, dialogue. If your character is someone who would naturally speak in clichés, then you would be correct in putting them into his/her mouth because it would add to characterisation.

Q. *What is a 'hackneyed phrase'?*

A. It means an over-used phrase such as 'at this point in time' or 'tip of the iceberg'. The expression itself sprang from the fact that the horses which were used to pull hackney carriages were usually tired, worn-out animals.

Q. *What are 'purple passages' and why should they be avoided?*

A. A so-called purple passage (or purple prose) is when a writer has gone over the top in describing something so that the meaning is actually obscured by too many words.

Chekhov said that the essence of good style is simplicity. Thus, suppose you described the sun filtering through the branches in a copse of hazel-nut trees in the following way: 'The hot golden ball of the sun pushed fiery fingers through the tangled canopy of the hazel-nut trees which stood unresistant yet defiantly resplendent in their autumn clothing.' I think that could be justifiably labelled 'purple prose' and you would be well advised to take a red pencil, cross it out, then rewrite, saying exactly what you meant in simpler form.

Q. *My novel has just been returned with a letter in which the editor said my writing was too self-conscious. What does that mean and how can I correct it?*

A. It is another way of saying it was over-written. Instead of telling your story simply, you probably embellished with the 'purple passages' previously described. A good exercise both to correct this novel and to help avoid repeating the fault would be to go through it with a red pencil, marking any passages which, for example, contained several adjectives or were in other ways too 'flowery' and rewrite using simple, straightforward language. When you have finished the exercise, go back and compare the two. The difference should be dramatic and obvious and your next story should be greatly improved.

Q. *I enjoy reading the classics like those by Jane Austen, Trollope, Hardy and so on, so why do I keep being told I mustn't write like them, today?*

A. The answer is simple: novelists of a hundred years or more ago were writing in the style of the times in which they and their readers were living. There can be little doubt that, if they were alive today and working as professional writers, their work would reflect the style of today. Remember, too, that when their novels were being published life was much slower and there were fewer distractions. Thus, longer descriptive passages, for instance, would be acceptable to readers or, as was often the case, to those listening to the story as many could not read. Modern-day readers mostly lead busy lives, watch TV and have time-consuming hobbies, so they want faster-paced fiction with plenty of action and not long descriptions of people and places.

Figures of Speech

Q. *I understand the need for original metaphors and imagery in fiction-writing but can you suggest any ways for producing them?*

A. It's a question of trying to see something in a different light, of describing it in a novel way which makes a piece of writing appear fresh and more alive. A simile is something likened to another as, for example, 'My love is like a red, red rose'. Robert Burns has already done that, so writers must now find another way of considering love. What about, say, 'My love is like an endless, flowing river'? At least that is different and may not have been said before.

A metaphor is more concrete, suggesting something actually *is* another object. One which has been used so often over the years that it is now a cliché is 'a heart of stone', used to describe a hard-hearted person. If you want to write about such a character, you need to find another way of getting across this trait. If you want to stick to using a metaphor, perhaps 'He had a heart of ironwood.'

Q. *I've heard the expression 'mixed metaphor' but I don't know what it means. Can you explain, please?*

A. It's when you use a metaphor (suggesting something *is* something rather than merely *like* it – feet of clay, for instance) and connect it with another completely different image. For example: He buried his head in the sand as he rode roughshod over everyone.

Adapting Style

Q. *I want to aim at the teenage market. Does that mean I must change my style?*

A. Yes, you will have to tailor it to suit your readership. The language used in both narrative and dialogue will be quite different from that in, say, a story aimed at a magazine for the retired. In writing for a teenage magazine, it is essential to use current slang to aid reader identification, otherwise you would quickly lose your readers.

Q. *What is 'house style'?*

A. Most publications have what is termed their own house style. This will include things such as whether they use single or double quotation marks for dialogue, and whether they are happy with the use of contractions (for example, don't) in narrative or insist on more formal language (do not). But there is no need to worry too much about this. Provided your piece is, in most respects, suitable for them, they will do any such necessary editing so that it fits their own house style.

Q. *I'm conscious of the need to improve my writing style and I very much admire that of one particular novelist. Would it be wrong to try to emulate his style?*

A. Most new writers, either consciously or unconsciously, to some extent tend to copy writers whose work they like, just as painters, down the ages, have painted 'in the style of'. In the end, though, you must develop your own individual way of putting words on paper if you are not to be a mere copyist. So be wary of slavishly following someone else's style.

Q. *When writing autobiographical pieces, does it matter if I keep on saying 'I' or should it be avoided, where possible?*

A. Obviously, use of the first person singular cannot be avoided in autobiographical material but, with careful structuring of the prose, it can be reduced. Aim to avoid its becoming too intrusive but don't worry unduly.

Q. *What is the current thinking of the use of 'he' when it is meant to indicate both male and female?*

A. This is a continually vexing question. Some publishers insist on he/she or s/he (though this becomes clumsy if used too often). Others prefer the masculine form throughout to include both sexes. Some writers will use the plural form of 'they' where it follows the singular pronoun 'everyone' (for example: Everyone will choose their own book), though this is not grammatically correct. It is really up to individual choice and the particular publisher's house style but it is a problem which is likely to be around for a long time.

Punctuation

Q. *Are there any rules or advice on the use of punctuation? For instance, is it permissible to use semicolons nowadays?*

A. There are certain definite rules for punctuation which, strictly speaking, should be observed but, far too often, are not. For example, a comma should follow an adverb: However, ... he said, warily, ... and so on. Commas should also enclose adverbial clauses: And, the next time, I expect you to ... ('the next time' being an adverbial clause of time). A simple test for the latter is to ask yourself if you could remove the clause altogether and the sentence would still make sense. For instance, remove the clause 'the next time' and you have a perfectly sensible sentence: And I expect you to .... A good, modern grammar book should help you, in this respect.

Remember, though, that fashions change. Today, there is a move towards reducing the amount of punctuation in prose in many publishing houses and periodicals. Both the colon and the semicolon are out of favour in most popular commercial fiction today, and it is generally preferable to make two sentences rather than separate one long one with a colon or semicolon.

Q. *Is there any reason why I shouldn't use dashes or exclamation marks in my writing?*

A. Too many of them scattered across a typescript produces a cluttered, fussy look which is unappealing to the eye.

Q. *What is an ellipsis?*

A. It is a row of three full-stops (...) used to indicate a speech tailing off.

Q. *Because I was taught at school never to use contractions in writing, I find it very difficult to break the habit now I'm trying to write commercially. Why should it have been considered wrong, while at school, and right, now?*

A. At school, especially some thirty or more years ago, it was considered correct to write in a formal style and not to use verb contractions (won't, can't, shouldn't, and so on). But this results in a stilted style which is generally disliked by today's readers. In an essay for a learned journal, it might be acceptable but certainly not in modern fiction. And definitely not in dialogue.

Q.   *What does the expression 'finding your own voice' mean?*

A.   It is another way of saying you need to develop your own style of writing.

Q.   *Are there any advantages to using the present tense in fiction?*

A.   The present tense can add immediacy to a work of fiction, by drawing the reader into the story as if the events were happening there and then in front of his eyes. It is a stylistic device which can be extremely effective if used judiciously. It has inherent dangers, however, one of which is the need to make sure you don't sometimes slip, unintentionally, into the more normal simple past tense. Generally speaking, if you start a story in the present tense (I am sitting here, writing this letter ...), you should continue in it and not switch to the past. A skilled novelist can sometimes switch tenses but they do so deliberately and for a specific purpose and in a definite manner. The beginner should be wary of this.

Q.   *What is the definition of a sentence?*

A.   Strictly speaking, it consists of a subject, an object and a verb and expresses a complete thought. However, on occasions, two or three words, or even a single one standing alone, is permissible and can be very effective.

Q.   *When I was at school we were taught never to start a sentence with 'And' or 'But' and never to end with a preposition. Does this rule still hold good?*

A.   No. In today's writing, which is more natural-sounding and faster-paced than that of years ago, it is often preferable to break a long sentence into two, starting the second part with a conjunction (e.g., and, but, then, also, although) or perhaps an adverb (for example: 'Even now, he remembered how he'd felt').

Similarly, ending a sentence with a preposition might well sound better than turning it round to be grammatically correct. For instance, 'That was something she'd often been warned about' sounds better than the more correct '... about which she had been warned, often'. An often-quoted example of the absurdity of rigidly sticking to such a rule of grammar was given by Winston Churchill to make just this point: 'This is the sort of English up with which I will not put.'

Q.   *What is symbolism and how should it be used?*

A.   It is a kind of literary shorthand. John Steinbeck described it as a kind of psychological sign language which is chosen to illuminate as well as to illustrate the whole. He talked about using, in *East of Eden*, a scarred forehead as a recurring symbol to suggest the maimed, the marked and the guilty – the imperfect. Iris Murdoch in *The Bell* used a trapped butterfly to symbolise the way her main character was trapped in marriage.

Many symbols are deeply embedded in our subconscious. For instance, white suggests purity and innocence; a tiger, animal strength; a house can denote security; and so on. By deliberately introducing symbolism into your writing you can add an extra dimension, an extra strength, to it.

Q.   *What is alliteration?*

A.   Alliteration is using words which begin with the same letter in order to create a particular effect. Titles using this device can be extremely effective, for example,

Granny Get Your Gun (which is also a pun on a famous musical, of course).

Q. *Can you explain how to use onomatopoeia?*

A. When you want to create an image of *sound* for the reader, you can often do so by using a word which resembles or imitates the actual sound in nature. For example, the word 'hiss' replicates what we understand to be a hissing sound. The careful choice of onomatopoeic words indicates a writer who has taken a lot of care with style.

Q. *Why should one avoid using adverbs?*

A. The over-use of adverbs is indicative of a lazy writer. It is often easier to tack an adverb on to a verb (he said, softly) rather than select a verb which does the work in one word instead of two (he whispered; murmured; muttered). Adverbs are an important part of our language but should be used judiciously, not sprinkled like confetti throughout a piece of writing.

SUMMING UP

You have decided on a working method which suits you, absorbed some of the basic rules of writing and considered some of the other aspects. You are now ready to move on and take an in-depth look at the various types of writing, any or all of which you may wish to try, either now or later.

The following sections will give you the opportunity to decide where your interests lie, initially at least, and put what you have learned into practice.

Writing Non-Fiction

Without doubt, the simplest thing to write – and the easiest to sell – is the straightforward factual or feature article for newspapers or magazines. But perhaps you are thinking of becoming a full-time journalist rather than a freelance, so how do you go about that? Or you may have a leaning towards writing for children. Each genre or type of writing will require different skills and approach.

This section will give you the opportunity of deciding which is likely to be the best non-fiction field for you. It will point out some of the commonest pitfalls, answer many of the questions asked by both new and established writers and set your feet firmly on the path towards your goal of seeing your work in print.

MAGAZINE ARTICLES

Q. *I have an idea for a feature article for a particular magazine. Should I query it first with the editor? If so, should I telephone or write?*

A. If your article is highly original or topical, by all means submit it. But many editors prefer an initial query letter rather than receiving the complete piece. It saves your

time, too, because if they don't want it for any reason –
perhaps they've just commissioned or accepted a
similar one – you can direct it to another publication.

It is not advisable to telephone an editor unless you
are known to them.

Q. *What fee could I expect for an article of, say, 800 words for a
small national magazine?*

A. It is impossible to say with any certainty but it is not
likely to be high. If you are just starting out, the important thing is to be paid for your work. Accept that you
will not be able to command as much as someone who
is well-known, and that small-circulation magazines
cannot afford large fees.

Q. *What is generally considered to be a saleable length for a magazine article?*

A. This depends on individual publications. Some magazines use longer, in-depth pieces while many prefer
shorter ones. A useful length to aim at is around 800
words.

Q. *Does it help to sell an article if I can provide photographs or
other illustrations?*

A. Often, yes. This is particularly so if the article in question lends itself to illustrations and if the magazine uses
them. Some magazines refuse to consider contributions
unless the author provides photographs/illustrations.

Q. *I've sold an article to a national magazine. As the research
took me quite a long time, I'm wondering if I could try to resell
the piece as it stands or should rewrite it and send it to another
publication?*

A. If you try to sell your article without rewriting, you must
offer Second British Serial Rights and inform the editor

where it has been previously published. However, the chances of selling it after it has already appeared in a national magazine are slim. Because there is no copyright in facts, provided you rework it, giving it a completely different angle or slant, it will then be a virtually new piece which you can submit to another publication, once again offering First British Serial Rights.

Q. *I notice that some magazine editors ask for ideas to be submitted, in the first instance. But could these be stolen and subsequently written up by someone on the staff?*

A. It is always possible that an idea could be stolen (there is no copyright in ideas) but not very likely. The advantage is that a decision on a basic idea can often be made more quickly than if a completed piece has to be considered.

Markets

Q. *Could you suggest some markets for the freelance writer?*

A. Apart from national magazines with which you should already be familiar, look at trade or specialist publications, many of which take freelance material. Ask friends and relatives if they know of a suitable in-house or trade journal and could let you see a copy. If you know anyone with an unusual or specific hobby, perhaps they take a relevant magazine which you could study. *Willings Press Guide*, available at larger public libraries, lists most of them.

A useful book which lists many available markets is *1000 Markets for Freelance Writers* (see Useful Publications, p. 200). But you, the writer, must always be on the look-out for potential new markets. For instance, when on holiday, buy the local or regional newspaper to see if there are any possible openings.

Q. *I've been submitting articles to various magazines for over a year but without success. I've studied the market carefully so I must be doing something wrong. Can you suggest what that might be?*

A. Assuming that the magazines you have submitted work to accept unsolicited material, the most likely explanation is that you haven't studied them in sufficient depth. You must analyse each one thoroughly so that you know its readership, the type of subject matter used and length of material printed.

For instance, do they use human-interest stories or factual pieces? If you've submitted the latter, were they so full of facts that they made dull, boring reading? Did yours have an interesting, unusual or topical slant? Were they, perhaps, too long for the particular market? The best advice is to concentrate on one or two specific publications for a while so that you know them inside out. Choose those which you enjoy reading yourself, and for which you honestly believe you can write.

Q. *I've researched a subject which I think would make an excellent feature article for a particular specialist magazine but, on checking through past issues, I see they printed one on similar lines about three years ago. Is there any point in writing it?*

A. The fact that they used a similar piece some years ago does not necessarily mean they would not consider another now, but it would probably need to be angled differently. Find another slant, then write to the editor, outlining your idea.

Q. *I'm making a serious attempt to break into the field of magazine articles. Ought I to aim for specific markets before writing a piece or can I write up a topic which interests me and which I've researched and then look round for somewhere to send it?*

A. The professional way is to look for a specific publication and then write your piece aimed at that particular one. If you do it the other way round, your slant or angle might not be right, nor the length, and you are inviting rejection. That is not to say there might not be several possibly suitable ones and, if one turns it down, then by all means try another. But do your homework, first, and you will improve your chances of selling one hundred per cent.

Q. *What is meant by a 'peg' to hang an article on?*

A. This is the topical angle which will improve its chances of acceptance. For example, an article on shoe-mending would be of little interest to most magazines, but a writer knowledgeable on the subject saw a potential 'peg' when Henry VIII's flagship, the *Mary Rose*, was raised from the sea bed and sailors' shoes were discovered in virtually pristine condition.

Q. *What is meant by the 'angle' of an article?*

A. Sometimes known as the 'slant', it is the specific aspect (or theme) of the subject you are writing about which will be dictated by the particular market at which you are aiming.

A useful maxim to keep in mind is: One theme, one article. Inform the reader in the first sentence what the aspect/slant/theme will be. For instance, suppose you wanted to write a piece about Christmas, this is such a vast subject you would have to decide on a specific *angle* or theme. That might be, for instance, food and its origins, or Christmas greenery (the fir tree, holly, mistletoe and so on). You must not include both in the same article.

Q. *When submitting an article to a magazine or newspaper, whom should I address it to?*

A. Usually, articles (as opposed to news items) should be sent to the Features Editor. If possible, try to find out his/her name and address it personally, though it isn't normally necessary to send a covering letter.

Terminology

Q.   *What is a 'glossy' magazine?*

A.   This is the term given to those more up-market period-icals, usually monthly, which have glossy covers and pages printed on high-quality paper.

Q.   *What is a 'pulp' magazine?*

A.   These are the lower end of the magazine market. They are printed on cheaper paper and are usually published weekly.

Why is Material Rejected?

Q.   *I've sent the same article to five different women's magazines, including two national glossies. Each one has rejected it but without indicating why. Does that mean it's badly written?*

A.   Not necessarily. Perhaps they were the wrong markets for the material or the length or treatment was not right for them.

Q.   *I'm getting really frustrated by having my work constantly rejected without being told why. Is there anything we writers can do to persuade editors and publishers to tell us why they have turned our work down?*

A.   Editors do not have time to write individual letters to would-be contributors so it would be virtually imposs-ible to reverse this situation. What you can (and should) do is make sure you have thoroughly studied each potential market before submitting work. You would be wise to put it aside for a week or two, then reread it as *objectively* as possible and see if you can possibly improve it before sending it out. After that, it is a question of practice and persistence until you achieve success.

Increasing Sales

Q. *How can I sell an article more than once?*

A. Simply by finding other angles which will make the material suitable for quite different magazines. In *Journalism for Beginners* (see Useful Publications, p. 199), Joan Clayton describes how a student sold four articles about a woman tiger-trainer written from four different angles. One was that a woman training tigers is highly unusual. Another was the controversial issue of whether training wild animals involves cruelty. A third had a regional slant, while a fourth dealt with the stress of constantly moving house for both the people and the animals.

Illustrations

Q. *Can I submit colour prints as illustrations for a magazine article?*

A. You should first check with the editor. Normally, either black-and-white prints or colour transparencies are preferred but some magazines accept colour prints, provided they are of good quality.

Q. *How necessary is it to provide illustrations for an article?*

A. It is said that a single picture is worth a thousand words. Certainly, good illustrations often help sell an article so it is always worthwhile providing some, if possible. If you can provide your own, it will be greatly to your advantage as you will own the copyright and won't have to share the fee you receive for publication.

Q. *How should I submit photographs to accompany my article?*

A. Make sure each is identified as belonging to you, either by lightly writing your name and address in pencil on the back or by sticking on a small address label. If you are sending more than one, number them so they can be linked to the caption sheet (which should accompany them), stating the subject of the illustration. And, most important, protect them with a piece of cardboard on both sides.

Q. *I need some illustrations to accompany my article but I'm not in a position to take the photos myself. Is there a source which might be able to provide them?*

A. There are commercial agencies which, at a price, will provide suitable photographs (see *The Writer's Handbook/ Writers' and Artists' Year Book* for names and addresses). Alternatively, you could employ a professional photographer but this could prove prohibitively expensive. Depending upon the subject of your article, museums and the relevant tourist board will often have suitable photographs for which there may or may not be a charge.

Q. *If illustrations to accompany my article are provided by someone else, what percentage of the overall fee will the photographer expect?*

A. This should be agreed between you before submitting your article to an editor. Most photographers will charge a flat fee for providing the pictures but you might be able to negotiate, say, a fifty/fifty split of the fee you receive from the particular magazine.

Q. *What proportion of the fee for an illustrated article would be in respect of the illustrations?*

A. Often, a larger proportion of the fee will be for the illustrations then for the actual article.

Q. *What is the correct size of photographs for submission to an editor?*

A. Normally, not smaller than 6 inches × 6 inches or 5 inches × 7 inches for black and white. Prints should always be glossy, not matt.

WRITING FOR NEWSPAPERS

Q. *I shall be leaving school, soon, and I'd like to become a journalist. How do I go about training to be one?*

A. There are two main routes into journalism proper (that is, not working as a freelance). One is to try to obtain a position as a junior reporter on a local/regional newspaper, many of which run their own training schemes. The other is via a course run by the National Council for the Training of Journalists. For further details, write to them at Carlton House, Hemnall Street, Epping, Essex CM16 4NL. There are a number of accredited colleges, around the country, which offer these courses.

There are also courses at some universities, leading to a degree in journalism, and at least one adult education authority (Westminster) runs evening classes in journalism, aimed at beginners.

Q. *What is the best way to get a regular slot in my local paper?*

A. First of all, aim to get your name and style known to the editor by contributing regularly to their letters page, for which, of course, you will not be paid. You could also offer to review plays, exhibitions, local charity events, club meetings and so on for them. Even if they already have a regular reviewer, there is always the possibility they might occasionally need someone to fill in. If the paper doesn't already have, say, a women's and/or a children's page, suggest one. Keep your eyes open for

items in the national press which might have a local
slant.

As often as practicable, get your name seen by the
editor: it will pay off eventually.

Q. *As a freelance journalist just starting out, how much can I
expect to be paid for material?*

A. That will depend upon the newspaper or magazine
which accepts it. As a beginner, you would not be eligible to join the National Union of Journalists so you're
unlikely to be paid at their rates. Besides, as someone
without a track record, you cannot expect to receive as
much as someone whose work in known. Magazines
with a small circulation will not be able to offer as much
as those with a large readership, and this also applies to
local or regional newspapers. Be prepared to be paid
less while you are serving your apprenticeship. Later
on, you will be in a better position to negotiate higher
fees.

Q. *How does a newspaper pay for news items?*

A. You will be paid lineage at whatever rate the editor
thinks you are worth, that is, so much per line of
printed copy.

Q. *I feel strongly about what might be considered a controversial
subject. If I write an article about it, is an editor likely to print
it?*

A. Whilst editors love controversial topics which spark off
a response in their readers, they do not want an *opin-
ionated* piece from someone who is merely standing on
a soapbox, preaching. Make sure you obtain as many
facts as possible to back up your stance on the subject.
If at all possible, include some pertinent quotes from
well-known or authoritative people.

Before embarking on such a piece, ask yourself: why would those readers be interested in my opinion? Then make sure you keep yourself well in the background. As C. P. Snow said, comment is free but facts are sacred.

Q. *Have you any advice for someone wanting to try their hand at journalism?*

A. First of all, ask yourself why you want to be a journalist. If you think it might be a rather exciting occupation, you would probably be better off doing something else, because there is a lot of hard, often boring slogging involved. Also, are you prepared to meet a deadline *at all costs*? If an editor is expecting a piece by a certain time, you cannot ring up to say it will be late because you're just off to meet your aunt off a plane, or you've gone down with the 'flu.

Reliability must be your watchword. You have to be utterly dependable, which also means relied upon to check facts so they are *always* correct.

Q. *What is the essence of writing good news stories?*

A. Succinct writing, plenty of facts, no opinions and no padding.

Q. *Are there are sacred watchwords for a journalist?*

A. Perhaps the main ones are accuracy, honesty, integrity and reliability.

Q. *Is there a formula for writing news stories?*

A. Copy for newspaper stories is always cut from the bottom up, so the vital elements should be in the first paragraph. These include the who, what, where, when, why and how. Rudyard Kipling referred to them in a famous verse in 'The Elephant's Child' in his *Just So Stories*.

I keep six honest serving-men
(They taught me all I knew).
Their names are What and Why and When
And How and Where and Who.

Start with the result of what you are reporting, then go on to list the other important facts so that, if your piece has to be cut because of lack of space, the salient bits will still be there.

Q.   *I want to have a crack at writing for my regional paper. How can I find out what style they like?*

A.   Obviously you must read the paper regularly and get a feel for its individual style but you could write (enclosing SAE) and ask for a copy of their style guidelines, if available. But there is no substitute for doing your own market study.

Journalistic Terms

Q.   *What is 'copy'?*

A.   This is the written material sent in to a publication by the writer or reporter.

Q.   *What is a sub-editor?*

A.   Sub-editors check facts, correct spelling and grammar, cut copy if necessary, and make sure the article is in house style before it goes to press.

Q.   *What is 'editorial'?*

A.   This is text in a newspaper or magazine which is not advertising material. It includes features, news reports, profiles and reviews.

Q.   *What is a byline?*

A. It is the writer's name at the head or foot of a piece, acknowledging him or her as the author.

Travel Writing

Q. *I'd like to write travel articles. Would it be possible to get an editor to sponsor me on a particular trip?*

A. It is very unlikely, if you are completely unknown, that you will find anyone willing to commission such an article. Nor is a travel company likely to give you a free trip in return for writing about it. If, however, you have been selling features on other subjects for some time, and now wish to break into this field, you could send query letters to suitable publications, offering your services. Also, try to get your name on as many public relations companies' lists as possible.

Whilst your chances are slight, nothing is lost by asking. But you would improve them considerably if you could first build up a portfolio of travel-linked pieces, to prove your capabilities.

Q. *I travel a great deal, independently. Could I break into what seems to be a closed-shop market for articles?*

A. There is always room for original, informative and entertaining travel pieces. However, it is wise to aim at first for the lower end of the market, where you stand a better chance of acceptance because competition is less fierce. Look for possible openings in 'freebie' magazines, some of which are available at London main-line stations and aimed at young backpackers. Study the travel pages in national papers, though, and if you think you have an unusual slant, send your piece in on spec.

Q. *A few years ago, I used to travel extensively and now I'd like to write about my experiences. But would they be considered out of date?*

A.   Probably. but you might be able to contrast them with travel today. Or you could write them up as part of your life story.

Book-Reviewing

Q.   *I'm a voracious reader and regularly read the book reviews in the national press. How do I go about becoming a reveiwer myself?*

A.   The first step is to get some experience. Write two or three reviews of recent books, then send them to the editor of your local paper and offer to review any new books for him. If he agrees, don't expect to be paid for your work, apart from being allowed to keep any review copies you receive.

INTERVIEWING

Q.   *I'm hoping to interview a local celebrity but, never having done this before, am not very confident. What preparations should I make?*

A.   Before you ask for an appointment, work out a basic plan. Make a list of things like why you think they should grant you an interview, the sort of piece you intend to write (that is, what the angle will be), possible places, dates and times for the interview suitable to both of you and, if you don't already have the information, the method of contacting the interviewee. And make sure you know the correct spelling of their name.

Once you have set up the arrangements, you need to do as much research into his/her background as is possible in the time available (you should have already done much of this). Then try to see the shape or structure of the proposed piece to help you with the next stage, which is to prepare your list of questions.

Once you have undertaken all these preparations, you will be more confident when you do the interview. Most people enjoy talking about their lives and careers, and you'll probably find all you have to do is make notes and throw in the odd question.

Q. *Is it necessary to use a tape-recorder when conducting an interview?*

A. No, but as a back-up to note-taking it is a definite advantage as it is all too easy to miss vital points when taking down notes and trying to listen at the same time.

Q. *I'd like to try my hand at interviewing but, as I am an unknown writer, would anyone agree to talk to me?*

A. With any type of writing, it is wise not to aim too high at the start. Look around for interesting but *ordinary* people living in your area who might be happy to be interviewed for your local paper. For instance, it could be someone raising money for charity in an unusual manner, opening an animal-rescue centre or performing a difficult or challenging feat of some kind. Once you have a few such interviews to your credit, you can widen your horizons and aim for subjects who are better known. Never be afraid to ask anyone for an interview. People in the public eye usually welcome publicity, as it enhances their career. As is often said, the only bad publicity is no publicity.

Q. *Would magazines or newspapers be interested in profiles on non-celebrities?*

A. Yes, provided the proposed subjects and their lives are sufficiently unusual and, when written up, would entertain or inform the readers.

Q. *I want to ask a local celebrity for an interview with the inten-*

tion of writing it up for publication. How should I approach the person involved?

A. If you know, or can easily find out, where they live, then write to them at their home address. State who you are, your credentials and which publication is interested in the piece. If it is impossible to contact them direct, perhaps your local paper would forward a letter; or, if he/she is a novelist, write c/o the publisher. But avoid telephoning, if possible, as the interviewee, faced with having to make a quick decision, might say, 'no'.

Q. *A quite well-known person living near me has agreed to my request for an interview. Before I go to see her, I'd like to sell the idea to a particular national magazine which I think might be interested. Are there any questions I should ask the editor, first?*

A. It would be worth enquiring if there is a particular slant he/she would like. For instance, if it is a women's magazine, the editor might be especially interested in a feminist angle. You also need to know the length required and the copy deadline.

Q. *When I'm writing up the interview, should I correct any grammatical mistakes the interviewee might have made?*

A. If you intend quoting verbatim and he/she made a glaringly bad grammatical mistake, then it would be wiser, and kinder, to correct it. However, often, a simpler and more politic way out of the dilemma might be to paraphrase, using your own, grammatically correct words.

Developing Books from Articles

Q. *I've written a series of anecdotal-type articles about people and events in my particular locality, and a few have appeared in the local press. Now I'm thinking of putting them together in* *book form, but have I prejudiced my chances of having a book published because they've already been printed?*

A. The fact that these articles have already appeared in your local paper would not of itself prejudice your chances of wider publication. But, because of their purely local flavour, it is unlikely they would have a wider, national appeal and you would have difficulty in interesting a general publisher in them. If you feel you must see them in book form, the best route would be to find a small, perhaps local, publishing/printing company and negotiate a price for however many copies you think you could sell over a reasonable period.

You would almost certainly have to undertake the marketing yourself, but as you would probably be restricted to a comparatively small area, this should not be too difficult. Bookshops in and around your locality, post offices, gift shops, stationers and so on, all might be willing to take a few copies on a sale-or-return basis.

Q. *Having had some success with short articles, I'd like to try my hand at a full-length book. How do I decide on a likely subject?*

A. First of all, ask yourself if there is any one area in which you consider yourself an expert. If there isn't, and you were intending relying on research, you would have an uphill task persuading a publisher that you could write a book that would be commercially viable. Initially, it is up to the author to sell himself to the publisher and to do that he has to have credibility.

However, assuming your published articles have been on topics on which you can write with authority, choose the one with which you feel most comfortable, for which you can obtain the most up-to-date relevant information and for which there is likely to be the biggest market.

Q. *I have an idea for a full-length book on a particular subject. Would it help me find a publisher for it if I could first sell one or two short pieces as articles?*

A. Yes. This would not only demonstrate your writing ability but also show your knowledge of your subject.

FULL-LENGTH NON-FICTION

Q. *I've an idea for a full-length non-fiction book. Should I write it first and then try to find a publisher, or find a publisher first?*

A. You should obtain a contract from a publisher *before* writing any non-fiction book. If you don't, you will involve yourself in a great deal of work which may never reach fruition.

Q. *How should I set about interesting a publisher in my idea for a specialist book on education, in a field in which I consider myself an expert?*

A. It depends on how much work you wish to undertake at this stage. You could send out an initial query letter, briefly outlining the proposed book and enclosing photocopies or tear-sheets of any relevant material you have had published. Include in your letter details of your experience in the field. All this will give the publisher an idea of your writing style and the depth of your knowledge. Because of the constant changes in fields like education, they will probably be interested only in a book which is either up-to-the-minute in content or general enough not to go out of date too quickly. You can send out as many query letters as you wish as it is unlikely you will receive favourable replies to them all.

However, if you feel you would prefer, and are able, to write a good proposal, you could go straight to that.

This stage is of paramount importance as upon it will depend acceptance or rejection.

Writing a Book Proposal

Q. *What is a book proposal and what should it include?*

A. This is the sales package on which will rest acceptance or rejection of your idea for a non-fiction book. It is the next – and vital – step after the query letters have gone out. If a publisher expressed an initial interest in the *idea* you put to them, they will have replied asking for a more detailed outline and specific examples of what will be included. Never rush this part of the project. There is no hurry (unless the idea is topical, in some way, and the publisher lets you know they would want to bring it out quickly, though this would be extremely unlikely) and it is better to take extra care, not only with content but also with the style of writing. Make sure there is not one grammatical or spelling error to prejudice your chances and present it correctly (see Presentation and Submission, p. 134).

It should include one or perhaps two chapters, plus a detailed, chapter by chapter outline of the rest of the book (allow a paragraph to a page for each chapter) and it is often useful to include an Introduction. The more information you give a potential publisher the more likely he is to be interested in your proposal.

You should have weighed up the competition from similar books currently available and considered in what way you can make your book different from those, convincing the publisher that *your* book will be better than any other on the same subject.

If possible, try to identify a gap in the market which your book could fill. You should suggest its likely readership and where it might be sold. For instance, do you attend conferences where you, as the author, might be able to sell copies? Finally, a prospective publisher will want to know its 'unique selling point'.

The more information you can provide at this point, the more likely it is that your book will receive serious consideration. A publisher should be able to make a decision fairly quickly once in receipt of all this.

There is no reason why you should not submit the detailed proposal to more than one publisher at a time, provided you make this clear to each of them.

Q. *How do I find a publisher for the full-length, non-fiction book I've just finished?*

A. It is always preferable to find a publisher (and receive a contract) before actually writing your book. However, as you have already completed it, first of all you should look at recently published books in libraries and book-shops in order to decide on which publishers to approach, then send them your typescript.

Q. *Can you give an example of a typical initial query letter to a publisher?*

A. Dear Joe Bloggs,

For the past fifteen years, I have been a practising (bee-keeper/stamp-collector or whatever) and have developed my own unique system of work/research, etc.). Although several general books on the subject are available, to my knowledge there is none which deals with it in the specific way which I have found both prac-ticable and simple. I believe there is a potentially large market for a book with this unique approach.

I enclose for your consideration photocopies of two of my articles which have appeared in ... in order to demonstrate my writing style.

I would be happy to produce a detailed outline of my proposed book, the suggested title of which is ..., should you feel it would be suitable for your list. I enclose a stamped addressed envelope for your reply.

Your sincerely,...

Collaborating/Ghost-Writing

Q. *Recently, a certain news story attained a good deal of media attention and I believe it would make a book. As the person concerned is not a writer, their story would probably have to be ghosted. How should I set about contacting the person involved, persuading them to accept me as their 'ghost' and then finding a publisher?*

A. Unless you have a track record in the writing world, it is unlikely anyone would consider giving you their story before you have interested a publisher in it. But, assuming you are already a successful freelance with at least one book to your credit, you could write to the person in question c/o the editor of the newspaper where you read the report. Simultaneously, you could start contacting a few suitable publishers to enquire if they might be interested, telling them of your writing experience. Time might be of the essence, especially if it is a situation currently in the news, in which case you would have to be prepared to work swiftly.

Q. *I've been told about a fascinating period in someone's life and would very much like to write it up as a book for them. I'm now contacting a number of publishers but wonder how we would split royalties in the event of its publication. What would be a fair split?*

A. A reasonable arrangement would be a fifty/fifty split of any profits. You would need to make sure the contract was clearly worded and all details agreed between the two parties before signing. You should consider if there might be foreign rights sold or possible film rights. If it got to the point of a publisher's being seriously interested, it would be worth considering using a literary agent to handle the business side of the deal.

An alternative way of dealing with this would be to approach the person in the news and suggest that you write their story on a fifty/fifty share of the profits *if*, once written, you are able to sell it to a publisher. Obviously, there is a much bigger risk, this way, that you will do a great deal of work with little or no reward at the end of it and it is not one to be recommended unless you are personally interested in the story.

Introductions

Q. *How much should I include in the Introduction to the full-length non-fiction book I'm working on?*

A. The Introduction should not be so long that no one will be bothered to read it but long enough to persuade potential readers the rest of the book will be worth reading – and buying. It will, perhaps, say why you felt the book needed to be written and why you think someone will benefit from reading it, hinting at what they will find in its pages. Somewhere in the region of a thousand words would be a reasonable length.

Biography

Q. *I'd like to write a biography of a person still living. How should I approach this person and would I have to obtain their permission to write it?*

A. It is far better to obtain the permission, and thus co-operation, of someone whose biography you want to write. You would then, almost certainly, have access to private papers and other documents which would be of considerable help to you.

An unauthorised biography (where permission has not been granted) is still possible, though you would have to be extremely careful about transgressing the law of libel should you write anything with which the subject disagreed. You would also probably have great difficulty in obtaining a contract from a publisher if it were unauthorised, in which case you could spend a lot of time for nothing.

Q. *I want to write a biography of someone now dead. Can I go ahead on my own or do I need to seek approval from the subject's living relatives?*

A. If you are prepared to write an unauthorised biography, you need not seek the approval of anyone. However, the book would stand a better chance of success if you were able to include material culled from letters, diaries and perhaps from interviews with relatives, if you obtained the co-operation of your subject's family or estate executors, in which case if would be an authorised biography. The one disadvantage of this is that they would almost certainly want to vet the book before publication and might object to parts of it and insist on their being taken out.

You will have to weigh that possible disadvantage against the advantage of being given access to more intimate material.

Q. *I've already started work on a biography but should I try to find a publisher before carrying on with it?*

A. Yes, unless you are so interested in your subject that you're happy to continue researching and writing, regardless of whether or not it appears in print. If you can't interest a publisher in the subject, you could do a good deal of work with no book to show for it.

Q. *I'm about to begin writing a biography and need to get information from members of the subject's family. Will I have to pay for it?*

A. Possibly, though this will depend on the people in question. But you need to have this made clear (and have something in writing) right at the start.

Autobiography

Q. *I've had a very interesting life and am considering writing my autobiography because I think a lot of people might like to read about it. Am I likely to find a publisher?*

A. That depends on how entertainingly you can write it. The fact that, in your opinion, your life has been an interesting one does not necessarily mean it will seem so to others, apart from your family and friends. Bear in mind, too, that the majority of published auto-biographies don't attempt to cover anyone's entire life but span a particularly interesting or unusual part of it. But even the simplest, most ordinary life story can, if told with humour, compassion and insight, prove to be a highly successful book. As so often, success lies in the telling. If your autobiography is so well written that the reader can't put it down until they have finished it, somewhere there will be a publisher who will jump at it. But you will probably have to persevere to sell it.

Q. *I have just finished writing my life story. What is the best way to go about getting it published?*

A. Approach those publishers who include autobiography in their lists. Send them two or three sample chapters (obviously, choosing those you think especially well written), together with an outline of the rest. If it has sufficient appeal, you might be lucky. But don't be too disappointed if you are not. Your family and maybe friends will doubtless enjoy it even if a wider audience never gets the chance to read it.

Q. *I'm about to start writing my autobiography. Must it be* *completely truthful or can I leave out bits or change some things I'd prefer people not to know?*

A. As it is your own life, such decisions are your own. But bear in mind that a too-sanitised version will inevitably lose something in interest.

Q. *I'd like to write my autobiography. I appreciate no one is likely to want to publish it but are there any advantages in writing it?*

A. There are several. It can prove therapeutic. It can validate your life at a time when you are experiencing a loss of identity, perhaps following retirement. It can provide entertainment for your family, helping them to know you better. It will also be a valuable piece of recorded social history, offering a bridge between the past and present for your immediate family.

Q. *How can I get my life story printed fairly cheaply? I'd like to have a few copies to give to various members of my family.*

A. Firstly, you will need to produce a typescript. If you aren't able to type yourself, you will have to find someone to do this for you. There are always people prepared to carry out this kind of work for a fee. Ask around in your locality or contact a typing agency that advertises in the area.

To have it produced in a simple book form, find a small publisher/printer and ask him to quote for however many copies you require. Ask to see examples of work done for other people before committing yourself.

Q. *In my autobiography, which I hope one day to get published, should I try to disguise the identity of various people in case of possible libel action if they didn't like what I'd said about them?*

A. If including such people will add to the entertainment value of your book and so you want to leave them in then you would be wise to disguise their identities as do other authors writing about their own lives. John Mortimer admits changing the name, sex and physical details of characters in his volumes of autobiography to avoid offence of any kind.

SUMMING UP

You have looked at the various kinds of non-fiction which you might consider trying your hand at. If, as suggested, you decide to start your writing with the easiest and simplest, the article, it should not be long before you see your first piece of work in print. But don't begin just yet. Later on in the book, you will find advice on how to study a particular market and on the correct way to present and submit material to an editor.

Writing Fiction

In order to become a fiction writer, above all, you need to be blessed with plenty of imagination. You must have the sort of mind that weaves stories around the people you meet or see in the street. You should be intrigued by overheard snatches of conversation, which make you curious about the people talking or those they were talking about. But, even if you have been gifted with a vivid imagination, to be successful in this highly competitive field, you need to know which *form* of fiction – short story, novel, children's stories, poetry or drama – you are happiest with.

In this section, you will have a chance to consider all these types of fiction, which should help you make up your mind which of them, if any, you want to try.

SHORT STORIES FOR MAGAZINES

Q. *Do some magazines have taboo subjects where fiction is concerned?*

A. Yes and no. Most women's magazines, for instance, will eschew anything unsavoury such as drug-taking, alcoholism, sexual perversions and so on. This is because their readers want to be entertained, to escape for a while from their problems, some of which may be connected with such subjects. Fiction in these magazines may be a little closer to reality, however, than it used to be and can touch on serious problems which affect many people, such as illness, divorce and bereavement, but these should be handled with care and sensitivity.

Q. *How do I find out if certain subjects are taboo?*

A. By studying several issues of whichever magazine you are aiming at. If, over a period of a few months, there is no reference to certain difficult subjects, it would be reasonable to assume these should be avoided.

Q. *I have a cupboard full of short stories that were either rejected or never submitted. Should I keep them, in the hope that they might appear in print one day, or just throw them away and write some more?*

A. Never throw away any writing. It is always possible the time wasn't right for a particular story when it was first submitted, or a new market may have since appeared for which it is more suitable. Also, as you become more skilled at your craft, you may be able to rewrite all or some of the stories more successfully. Perhaps now is the time to take them out of the cupboard, reread them objectively and see which excite you sufficiently to want to work on them some more.

Q. *How long is a short story?*

A. Strictly speaking, a story should find its own length, but for purposes of selling this will be dictated by a specific market's requirements. However, a popular length is around 2500 words.

Q. *Do true-life or 'confession' stories have to be actually true, or can they be pure fiction?*

A. They are always fiction, but are *based on* real-life situations so they have that essential ring of truth. There are not as many magazines printing this type of story today as there used to be, and the stories are not always told in the first person.

Q. *What is a 'twist-end' story?*

A. Sometimes known as the story with a 'twist-in-the-tail', it was popularised by the American writer O. Henry (in fact, that was a pseudonym: his real name was William Sydney Porter) around the turn of the century, when he wrote a large number of them. Currently, they are back in vogue in many magazines.

They are shorter than most short stories (often known as the 'short short') and depend for their impact on the 'twist'. To write them successfully, it is necessary to know the end and work backwards when plotting. The secret is to surprise the reader without cheating. It is essential to plant clues, or at least hints, throughout, so that when he reaches the end he will give a wry smile and realise he should have guessed! The ending, though a surprise, must be the logical, inevitable outcome of events. Two famous stories in this genre are Maupassant's 'The Necklace' and O. Henry's 'The Gift of the Magi', both character-led as all good fiction should be. 'The Necklace' revolves round a vain, superficial woman, while 'The Gift of the Magi' is about the unselfishness of deep love. In other words, there is still a theme, and the story has something to say.

Q. *What are the crisis points in a short story?*

A. The word 'crisis' comes from the Greek *krisis* and means 'decision'. The crises in a short story involve the main character, through developing and worsening circumstances, being forced to make a decision, to take some action. They are the obstacles (and the bigger the better) placed in your character's path, leading up to the worst of all, the climax. As this means 'ladder' (from the Greek *klimax*), one can see that the climax is the top of the ladder or storyline.

Q. *What is meant by 'slice-of-life' stories?*

A. They enjoyed a vogue a few years ago, and make a brief reappearance from time to time. They have scarcely any plot or storyline but depend for effect on re-creating incidents and events which are true to life and have little recourse to fictionalising. Short stories of this nature were sometimes called 'boneless wonders'. They are not popular with editors and are therefore likely to be difficult to sell.

Q. *How important is the ending of a short story?*

A. A *satisfactory* ending is of the utmost importance in any work of fiction but especially so in a short story. If a novel is well written, a reader might perhaps forgive a disappointing ending but a short story with a weak ending may well never get published. For instance, to allow a coincidence to bring about the resolution would ruin what might otherwise have been a good story. Suppose your main character, faced with a deepening dilemma, was killed in a car accident, thus allowing him off the hook of solving his problem by his own efforts, the reader would be justified in feeling cheated. Spend sufficient time *planning* the storyline, including the climax and the dénouement (or resolution), and you are far more likely to succeed than if you do not.

Q. *Do magazine stories have to have happy endings?*

A. Not necessarily, though, particularly in women's magazine fiction, it will be happy, or at least 'hopeful' as the intention is to uplift readers not depress them. But never make it contrived merely to produce a happy ending. It should be the right one for that particular story.

Q.   *Is a short story more than just a short piece of fiction? Could you define it, please?*

A.   It is more than just a short piece of fiction. Self-evidently, it is short in length but it is also a definite genre. Truman Capote said that it is the most difficult and disciplining form of prose writing there is (note the word 'disciplining'). William Trevor, a celebrated short-story writer, has described it as being 'the art of the glimpse'. In *The Summing Up*, Somerset Maugham says that he saw it as 'a narrative of a single event, material or spiritual'. The key phrase is 'single event'.

There are many and varied definitions of the short story. Nancy Hale in *The Realities of Fiction* likens it to a precision watch. It is akin to taking a day trip, whereas the novel is more like going on a fortnight's holiday.

Q.   *How many characters should there be in a short story?*

A.   There is one main character and, in the average-length story, there should only be two or three others. It is wise to limit the number to no more than five at most. As the story will revolve around the main character, who will have a specific problem to resolve or goal to achieve, introducing too many minor characters will reduce the story's power and effectiveness.

Q.   *I've heard the Greek unities are important in connection with short story writing. Could you explain what they are?*

A.   They are the unities of time, place and action, which were widely used in classical drama (the unity of action was delineated in Aristotle's *Poetics*; the other two are later additions). As the modern short story evolved as a

76

genre, it came to be seen that, by observing at least two of these unities, the resulting tight structure made it more effective.

The unity of time means the story should cover a short time-span from beginning to end (a useful guide, here, is not longer than a week), though this does not include flashbacks. The unity of action involves telling the story from the viewpoint of one character (the main character) only. The unity of place is maintained if the story opens and closes in the same location. For example, if a story opens with a scene in a village hall, if it ends in the same hall, the unity of place will have been observed.

As a general rule, it is wise to observe the unities of time and action, at least. It is wise to leave experimenting and ignoring a structure which demonstrably works until you have become a skilled, and successful, short-story writer.

Q. *Is it wrong to start a short story by telling the reader something about the main character's background?*

A. All fiction should start close to a high point of interest, at a point of change in the life of the main character, when something is happening or is about to happen which affects the status quo. In a short story, especially today when they seem to be becoming even shorter, there is little time or space in which to establish the background, describing the events which led up to the start of the story proper: otherwise, it might hold up the action and you would be in danger of losing your reader.

For example, suppose your story is about a fifty-year-old executive suddenly being made redundant and how he copes with it. If you start by describing how he worked hard at school and passed all his exams, went to college, started work and stayed with that same firm all his life *before* we are given a hint of the blow that was about to befall him, we might lose interest and never read any further.

There is a truism that it is wise to jump straight into a short story as if in midstream. Another is that, if you cut off the first third of your story, it will probably be at about the right starting point. The important thing is to capture the reader's interest, immediately, and make sure you keep it.

NOVELS

Q. *Are novels always first published in hardback?*

A. Traditionally, novels were first published in hardback, and then followed by the paperback edition some six months or so later. Today, however, the practice of paperback-only publishing is growing because the cost of production is considerably lower and more people buy them than hardbacks. In fact, some imprints are exclusively paperback.

Q. *What is a novella? Is it a short novel?*

A. It is a hybrid – somewhere between a short story and a novel. In length, it is from about 20,000 words to, say, 40,000. An example is Hemingway's *The Old Man and the Sea*. As an artform it is not popular, today, and it would not be advisable for a new writer to consider it. A well-known and prestigious writer might get one published but it would be almost impossible for anyone else.

Q. *Must a romantic novel have a happy ending?*

A. Yes. But there is a difference between a romance and a love story. The former is a specific category novel and the reader expects that, whatever the vicissitudes the heroine experiences throughout its pages, she and the hero will come together at the end with all misunderstandings cleared up and will live happily ever after. In a love story, as in the famous book of the same name by Erich Segal, this may not necessarily be the case. However, if you are aiming at the popular, commercial women's fiction market, you would be wise to give your story a conventional happy ending, whatever sad events take place beforehand.

Types of Novel

Q. *What are category novels?*

A. The main categories are: whodunnit/crime; thriller/ psychological thriller; adventure; western; contemporary romance; historical romance; historical; gothic/ romantic suspense; science fiction/fantasy; family saga; contemporary women's saga or Aga saga; woman/child in jeopardy. The last two categories are comparatively new and currently enjoying a vogue, while the straight historical and gothic/romantic suspense continue to be out of fashion in the UK, but remain popular in the USA.

Q. *Do specific categories require specific word lengths?*

A. Yes, generally speaking. They are:

- Contemporary romance: 50,000–55,000
- Historical romance: 85,000–95,000
- Sagas – family/regional/period: 120,000–150,000
- Aga sagas: 85,000–100,000
- Mystery/whodunnits: 75,000–95,000
- Science fiction: 75,000–95,000
- Fantasy: 120,000–150,000
- Erotic fiction: 60,000–85,000 (but check different imprints)
- Woman in jeopardy/psychological thrillers: 100,000–120,000

Q. *I've heard that you stand a better chance of success in the field of full-length fiction if you aim for a specific category. Why is that?*

A. It is because book-selling and book-publishing are much more market-orientated than they used to be. In bookshops, paperback novels, in particular, are displayed in labelled sections, making it easier for the purchaser to choose. Books are bought in specific categories from the distributors. Thus, a new writer trying to break into print will improve his chances of success if his novel fits readily into a category. But never try to mould a story to a category it is patently not right for or you could spoil what might have been a really good book.

Historical Novels

Q. *I'm working on a historical novel. Should I introduce people who actually lived as characters in my book?*

A. This is entirely a matter of choice. To do so, of course, can add a welcome verisimilitude to a historical novel.

Q. *I'm writing a historical novel and have been told they're not in fashion at present. Is this true and are there fashions in writing?*

A. Yes, fashions come and go in the world of fiction as in other fields and, unfortunately, the straight historical novel has been out of favour with publishers for quite some time. However, there are signs that it is about to make a come-back and perhaps, when yours is ready for submission, that time will have arrived. Historical *romances*, though, continue to sell, so it might be worth considering if it is possible to give it a romantic focal point to make it more saleable. But, in any case, a cracking good novel, of whatever category, will usually find a publisher.

Q. *I intend writing a historical novel and I'm wondering how much research I should undertake before I begin.*

A. You should be thoroughly familiar with the period before you attempt to set a novel in it. If you don't already know it in depth, do sufficient research before you start writing to enable you to bring it to life for your reader. There must be no glaring anachronisms which would destroy the illusion of period you are building up. For example, having a character from the fifteenth century utter expressions like 'How did he get on with his wife?' or 'I must be off now' or 'No way!' would be completely wrong, as would introducing terms such as 'biscuits', 'fortnight' or 'baby-sitter'. Only you will know when you have done enough, but there is also the danger of spending too much time on research and putting off starting the actual writing.

Erotic Writing

Q. *Is it true that erotic fiction is growing in popularity? How would you define it?*

A. There is a growing market for so-called erotic writing within the sphere of women's popular fiction, though it is small compared with other areas. It might be termed 'soft porn' and seems to have started as a challenge to what was previously an all-male province.

Undoubtedly, there is money to be made from this new genre (which is written almost exclusively by women) but anyone who feels uncomfortable writing mainly about sex would be wise to leave it alone and concentrate their efforts on other forms of fiction.

Q. *Does a novel have to contain explicit sex in order to be successful?*

A. No. This is a myth which seems to have grown up because some 'raunchy' novels have become best-sellers. Unless sex scenes are an integral part of your story, don't put them in.

Young Adult Novels

Q. *Is there a market for the teenage novel?*

A. Yes, although it is a more restricted one than that for adult fiction because many teenagers progress straight from children's to adult fiction. This genre is often known as young adult fiction, and it deals specifically with problems young people can relate to: family break-up, experimenting with drugs, running away to the big city, being pressured into sex at an early age, believing that romance, marriage or having a baby is the solution to their emotional problems, and so on. To succeed in this genre, the writer must be able to sympathise and empathise with young people experiencing all the difficulties of growing up in a complex world.

Jane Gardam is one writer who is able to re-create the world of young people with understanding, sympathy and humour. Probably the best-known novel about a teenager is J. D. Salinger's *The Catcher in the Rye*. From time to time publishers bring out imprints aimed specifically at young adults so, if this is where your interest lies, keep an eye out for these.

Q. *Are there any popular themes in today's young adult fiction and how can I find out what they are?*

A. As with any age group, themes which strike a chord with teenagers are those to which they can relate. Thus, any social problems which affect young people can safely be used as background to novels for young adults. For instance, being brought up in a single-parent family; moving to a different part of the country because of a parent's job; one's first boyfriend or girlfriend; pressure to do well at school; perhaps running away from home for various reasons. All these and many more provide a basis on which to write a novel which will appeal to teenagers.

Formula Novels

Q. *What is a formula novel?*

A. In a sense, all popular fiction is based on formula, though it rather depends on what you mean by the term. Popular, commercial fiction will be more formulaic than, say, mainstream fiction, but that does not mean it is less well written. An American literary agent once said that, if we analysed what was going on beneath the surface of classic novels, we would find the same formulas or tricks of the trade.

The main character always has a strong driving force which motivates his/her actions (for example, in Gustave Flaubert's *Madame Bovary*, the eponymous heroine desperately wants release from boredom and shortage of money). He/she will be in conflict with another section of society and face personal challenges. The main character's basic situation will continue to worsen throughout the novel, he/she standing to lose something important to them. There is always an inevitable climax, followed swiftly by the resolution or dénouement.

Q. *Is it possible to set out deliberately to write a best-seller and, if so, what is the formula?*

A. Assuming the question refers to popular, commercial category novels, which embrace most best-selling fiction, no doubt there are a few talented writers who can set out to write one or more – and succeed. First of all, however, they will have analysed in depth those currently successful novels in the genre in which they intend to write.

To some extent, the formula is the same for all commercial novels. They require a strong, dramatic storyline with a direct, uncomplicated narrative structure, a high proportion of dialogue and a fast pace with plenty of conflict. One best-selling author suggests that there should be a page-turning high point every three or four pages and a major crisis every twenty or thirty pages. There is almost always a happy ending, with the main character coming out on top, having achieved his or her goal in spite of all obstacles.

Fact/Fiction: Faction

Q. *Is it true that all first novels are autobiographical?*

A. This is a generally held belief, probably because most novelists draw upon their own experience ('write about what you know') for their first book. Not that all the events, incidents or characters portrayed will have been taken from real life – they will only have provided the germ from which the story sprang.

Q. *Can I write my autobiography and then try to sell it as a work of fiction?*

A. No. Although fiction can be (and often is) based on real-life events, a novel must be structured in such a way that it moves inexorably towards a climax and satisfactory ending, whereas life has no such precise structure.

Q. *I want to write about something strange and incredible which actually happened to a member of my family. Can I write it up as fiction?*

A. Yes. However, bear in mind that truth *is* often stranger than fiction and that, as bestselling novelist, P. D. James, once put it, 'Art is a rearrangement of reality', while T. S. Eliot suggested we can bear only so much reality. Thus, whilst you can certainly use an actual incident or event as the *basis* for your story, it is unlikely to work if you try to write it exactly as it happened.

Take the event itself, then ask yourself questions. What if ...? Suppose that ...? What if something else had resulted from that particular incident rather than what did transpire? Suppose that, instead of that person reacting as they did, they behaved differently? In this way, you will develop a plot/storyline which will be much stronger and, oddly, more believable than if you had stuck to the truth.

Q. *Isn't fiction-writing largely a matter of inspiration? Surely, to have to conform to rules of any kind destroys the imaginative, creative part of anyone's work?*

A. There is something of a misconception, here, as to the nature and meaning of rules or guidelines, whichever you prefer to call them. They have evolved, over time, as providing the best means of telling a good story. Without some kind of structure, no work of art (and this includes all types of writing) is likely to be successful.

Writing a Synopsis

Q. *I know one should include a synopsis of a novel when approaching a publisher but how long should it be and how much of the story should be included?*

A. Synopsis writing seems to cause problems for many people. Most publishers/agents want no more than about three or four A4, double-spaced pages. The aim of a synopsis is to persuade the publisher that he *must* consider the novel for his list. It should state when the action is taking place (for example, in the present, the 1800s or in the future) and over how long a period (two weeks, two years, forty years and so on). It should give details of the background and setting (for example, a small farm on Dartmoor, a market town in the North of England) and should briefly describe the main characters.

A synopsis should always be written in the present tense. A simple but effective method is to outline the main action, chapter by chapter, allowing one or two sentences for each chapter, as in the following example:

Chapter One: Laura Weston is shocked to learn that her oldest and closest friend, Janice, is dying. This forces her to take stock of her own life.

Chapter Two: At the funeral, Laura meets Janice's brother, Simon (with whom she had once been in love), for the first time in twenty years. She realises she is still attracted to him.

Continue in this way to give an outline of the entire novel, so the publisher knows you have thought through the storyline to the end.

Q. *I'm about to submit the first few chapters and a synopsis of my novel to a publisher. If they are interested, will I be expected to stick to the synopsis?*

A. No. A publisher only wants to see if the author knows the direction the novel will take. He knows from experience the storyline is likely to change as the novel progresses.

PRACTICAL MATTERS

Q. *Can chapters in a novel vary in length?*

A. Yes, though it is probably wiser to keep them fairly uniform in length. In some categories, such as contemporary romance, such uniformity is definitely preferred.

Q. *How many chapters should there be in a novel?*

A. There is no rule about this. There can be as many as you feel right for the book. Sometimes a book is divided into sections rather than actual chapters.

Q. *What is the average print run for a first novel?*

A. Around 2000 copies would probably be an average hardback print run for a first novel.

Q. *Why can't I write what I want to write and expect to be published?*

A. These are two separate issues. Anyone may write whatever they wish but if they want to see their work in print it must, with rare exceptions, also be something which a reader will want to read. It is often difficult for the beginner to appreciate that what he is producing, if his aim is to see it in print and be paid for it, is, in fact, a commodity. The days of the dilettante writer and indulgent publisher are long gone. Publishing is a commercial enterprise and, unless the public is prepared to pay for its products, it will quickly go out of business. Perhaps unfortunately, few publishers are now prepared to risk money on fiction which might be considered too *avant-garde* for most tastes and prefer to stick to tried and tested forms.

If your goal is to appear in print, as opposed to writing what you yourself want, then you need to study the market, look at current trends and try to stay reasonably close to them. That is not to say, however, that there is no room for originality and for the individual voice – there is. Indeed, it is a quality all editors and publishers are looking for. The problem lies both in producing a well-written, exceptional, original story and in convincing a publisher it will be well received. Once an author is established, of course, the latter will be that much easier.

Q. *Is there an advantage in having your book published in hardback?*

A. A hardback edition carries with it a certain prestige and is more likely to be reviewed, especially by leading newspapers, than a paperback. The latter, however, is likely to be more financially rewarding – which may outweigh other considerations – and the practice of going straight into paperback is growing.

Q. *How many copies sold make a novel a best-seller?*

A. It will vary from publisher to publisher, but something in the region of 10,000 copies in today's commercial climate.

Q. *What is a library edition of a novel?*

A. A book published solely for purchase by libraries and which will not ordinarily be sold in bookshops.

Q. *Are there any rules which, once learned, will ensure success?*

A. Unfortunately, it isn't as simple as that, though learning some generally accepted rules of technique are certainly an aid to achieving success. For instance, understanding how to write effective dialogue, how to build up tension and suspense and using viewpoint correctly all are important elements of good fiction-writing. For more information, on this, see Section Five.

Q. *What is a* roman-à-clef?

A. It means, literally, 'novel with a key'. It is a novel in which one of the characters (probably the main one) is a thinly disguised, well-known living person. But one should be very wary of attempting this, bearing in mind the laws of libel.

Q. *I've heard there are only a certain number of basic plots for the fiction writer to use. Is this true?*

A. A man called Georges Polti, expanding on a theory by Carlo Gozzi (author of the story of Turandot on which Puccini's opera is based), discovered and classified thirty-six dramatic situations. He maintained that all possible plot situations are variations of these. Subsequently, they were produced in book form under the title *The Thirty-Six Dramatic Situations* (see Useful Publications, p. 200).

Q. *I have what I think is a brilliant idea for a novel but I know I'm not skilled enough to write it myself. If I approached a published novelist, is it likely he or she would be interested in it and, if so, how would we split the royalties on the finished book?*

A. It is extremely doubtful that any writer would consider an idea by someone else. Even if the basic idea appealed, it is unlikely the story would develop exactly along the same lines as you envisage, which could lead to disagreements. Also, even if there were complete agreement between you over the resulting novel, it would be difficult to decide on what would be a fair split of royalties because the actual writing would entail a great deal of hard work in comparison to merely thinking up the idea. Better by far try to write the book yourself, and hope you produce a successful one.

Terminology

Q. *What is meant by the term 'reader-identification'?*

A. The ultimate goal of every fiction-writer is to persuade readers to suspend disbelief so they experience vicariously the events taking place within the pages. In other words, the readers identify with the main character as he/she struggles to overcome all the obstacles in his/her path – copes with tragedy, falls in love, suffers or rejoices throughout the story unfolding. When, against all odds, the main character wins out (as they do in the vast majority of fiction), the readers will sigh with satisfaction or maybe even weep for joy along with the character.

If your characters are real-life ones, not cardboard cut-outs, the situations you have put them into are credible and you imbue them with emotions most people have experienced – grief, happiness, anger, loneliness, love, rejection, being misunderstood and so on – then they are more likely to identify with them. The more you, the author, are involved with your characters, the more you engage closely with them, the more you will bring about that vital element of reader-identification.

Q. *What is 'immediacy'?*

A. This is difficult to define. It is closely linked with reader-identification. It is the feeling the reader should have of being there as the events take place; of being so caught up in the story that he totally suspends his disbelief until the end is reached. It is a key element in fiction-writing but comes about as a by-product of all the other important techniques.

Q. *What is meant by 'theme'? Is it different from plot? How important is it?*

A. The theme of a story can be loosely interpreted as meaning its implied message: that is, what it is *saying*. For instance, if the plot revolves round a power struggle, the theme might be that, in the end, power corrupts. If it is about survival against all odds, it might be that the will to survive is man's strongest instinct. This, surely, is what *Gone With The Wind* is about? The theme of *Othello* is that, ultimately, jealousy destroys.

Theme is not the same as plot. Plot is the relating of the incidents which result in proving the theme (or premise, as it is sometimes called). If your story has no theme, it will have nothing to communicate to the reader and, in effect, will be 'much ado about nothing'.

In essence, it is the ultimate goal or purpose of the story – your reason for writing it, even if you do not realise this, at the start. Lajos Egri, in *The Art of Dramatic Writing*, suggests that a premise is no more than a shorthand way of saying that 'character through conflict leads to a conclusion'. So if possible try to identify the theme, as this should help you write a more powerful story.

WRITING FOR CHILDREN

Q. *I have three children of my own (now grown up), so would it be easier for me to start with writing for children?*

A. This is not an easy option and, if you are out of touch with young children, it is likely to be difficult to achieve success. Aspiring writers sometimes make the mistake of deciding to begin here, harking back with nostalgia to either their own or their children's childhood. They forget that times have changed. Today's children have different tastes and interests and tend to be more sophisticated, having been exposed to television, bringing the world into the living room, to videos and computer games, to far more foreign travel, not to mention the rapid expansion of the space age, which earlier generations were not.

Before deciding, ask yourself *why* you want to write

for children rather than for adults. Unless the answer is that you have an overpowering desire to do so and you are in constant touch with them, as a teacher, parent or grandparent, then you should think again.

Q. *I want to write for children. Are there any subjects which are 'out' and any which are 'in'?*

A. Fashions change in children's fiction as in any other genre. For this reason, if for no other, it is essential to keep abreast of what is being published *now* in this field. Fairies, elves and gnomes are definitely out and will probably remain so, their place in children's literature having been taken by dinosaurs, monsters, beings from outer space and suchlike. Dragons (akin to dinosaurs), witches (not necessarily wicked), unusual animals which think and talk like humans (but not in a twee or sentimental way) seem to be perennially popular. Similarly, stories about children being involved in believable adventures or solving mysteries have never gone out of fashion.

As with other forms of fiction, originality is the keynote. Come up with exciting, new characters in modern-day situations and you are much more likely to succeed than if you write about what was in favour years ago.

Q. *I've been writing children's stories for more than two years, so far without success. I read them to my small grandchildren and they seem to love them, so why can't I sell them?*

A. The problem probably lies in the fact that the children know and love you (the same often applies to teachers). They are also getting extra attention by having you read to them, so are more likely to sit still and listen. The test is whether an audience who did not know you would find hearing the stories (or reading them for themselves) equally appealing.

By all means try out your stories on children you know but don't omit your market study. Remember that you have to persuade publishers and editors as well as parents and librarians that a story or novel is suitable for today's readership and is likely to appeal to them. It has to be seen as a commercial proposition or it won't be accepted. For your work to appear in print publishers have to risk their money and they will only do so if they believe there will be a reasonable return.

Q. *Is writing for children different from writing for adults? Should I aim at a specific age group?*

A. Yes and no. Obviously, the story will be shorter than for an adult novel but, just as with adult fiction, it must have a strong storyline, plenty of action, lively dialogue and a theme.

It is vital to know which age group you are writing for *before* you put pen to paper. Take a look at children's books in any library or bookshop and you will see they nearly always indicate the age range they are suitable for.

There are stories (mainly picture books) for the very small child, followed by those for pre-reading age, say from three to five. After that, there are early readers for children up to about seven, followed by longer, slightly more involved stories suitable for up to eleven-year-olds. Once a child is eleven and is assumed to have reached a high degree of reading competence, the final category before they go on to adult fiction is known as young adult fiction or teenage novels. These can be anything up to 40,000 words or even, occasionally, longer.

Q. *I'm a teacher of young children and feel I could produce good books for that particular age group. I'm thinking, in particular, of those with not much text and plenty of pictures. How should I approach a publisher offering to write the storyline only?*

A.   This type of book looks deceptively easy to write but it is not. But publishers are always on the lookout for good new writers who can come up with original ideas which will appeal to children of this age group. What they do not want are rehashes of stories already in print.

    If you believe you have a story which is different and which would be suitable for very young children, submit it in the usual way and state in your covering letter that you are a teacher and, therefore, in constant touch with that particular age group.

Q.   *Are there any do's and don'ts which it would be useful to bear in mind when approaching a children's publisher?*

A.   Don't try to over-sell yourself and your book by suggesting it would have merchandising spin-offs such as T-shirts, toys and so on. Don't say that your book is better than the rubbish you see on bookshelves in shops and libraries (self-praise is no recommendation and you are implying that that particular company is guilty of publishing rubbish). Lastly, make sure your manuscript is correctly presented (see Presentation and Submission, p. 134).

Q.   *I'm planning a children's book aimed at seven- to eleven-year-olds. What age should my characters be?*

A.   Your main character should be about eleven. Make your characters slightly older, rather than younger, than your intended reader of whatever age group because they usually prefer to read about exploits of children older than themselves.

Q.   *Are there any fatal traps to avoid when writing for children?*

A.   Perhaps the worst one is writing down to your intended reader. You must always respect your audience. Try to get into their minds, seeing things from their perspective rather than through the eyes of an adult. This way, you will avoid being twee which is, perhaps, the worst fault of many would-be children's writers.

Q. *As a teacher in junior school, I am constantly frustrated by the lack of suitable books to help backward readers. I have been trying to fill the gap by writing my own stories, which have been received well. Might a publisher be interested in them? If so, how should I go about approaching one?*

A. If you have identified a genuine gap in the market, it is likely you have a saleable proposition, perhaps for a series aimed at children with reading difficulties. Write to any educational publishers of this type of book, briefly outlining your proposal, telling them of your experience as a teacher and why you have been producing your own material to overcome this lack. While waiting for a reply, start preparing a detailed proposal for a series of these books, stating age of readership aimed at, length of books, subject matter and any other relevant details.

Q. *Are there any particular characteristics to bear in mind when writing for different age groups?*

A. With the two main groups of readers (as opposed to pre-readers), the main characters in stories aimed at six- to nine-year-olds should overcome a fear or simple problem of the kind that the reader would be able to identify with. For the older reader (aged eight to twelve) the main character will be rather more complex, reacting to his/her world, to his own personal problems and to the people around him. He/she will be developing a definite personality in the same way as the reader will be.

Remember to give the main character in your stories an urgent problem, one which is both vitally important to him/her and also one which children of that particular age would recognise and be able to solve. *Never* have an adult solving it for them.

Q. *I've written a children's book and wish to illustrate it myself. Should I send my original drawings to the publisher, together with the text?*

A. If you are an artist of *professional* standard, you could include some sample drawings with your typescript. However, most publishers will have their own stable of professional illustrators so the chances of their using an author's drawings are not very high.

DRAMA

Q. *Should serious drama have a specific function?*

A. It has been said that drama should involve the exploration of a moral dilemma. Another way of putting it might be that it should leave an audience with something to think about.

Q. *Does writing a stage play differ from writing a radio play?*

A. Yes. For one thing, in a stage play the audience can *see* action as it takes place, so doesn't have to be *told* what is happening. There will probably be less actual dialogue than in a radio play, for the same reason, and there are obviously more constraints on scene-setting on stage than on radio.

Because the two media are quite different, it is important to consider the various constraints before deciding which to write for.

Q. *A novel I read years ago would, I believe, make a wonderful play for either radio or TV and I'd like to try to adapt it. Can I do this without getting permission from the author?*

A. No, you would have to obtain permission, otherwise you would infringe the law of copyright. Write to the author c/o the publisher.

Q. *I'd like to write a play but rarely go to the live theatre. Would I stand a better chance of success trying one for radio?*

A. Provided you listen regularly to radio drama, you should have far more chance of success in this medium than you would in one of which you have little knowledge.

Stage Drama

Q. *Have you any advice for someone who wants to try their hand at writing plays for live theatre?*

A. Go to the theatre as often as possible and, even more important, join a local theatre company in any capacity whatsoever, not necessarily as an actor. That way, you will absorb some of the techniques of what does and does not work on stage.

Q. *I've recently completed a stage play. What is the next step towards getting it published?*

A. There is a truism that a play is not a play until it has been performed, so your next step should be to persuade a theatre company, either an amateur group or your local repertory company, to put it on. If they agree, it will prove invaluable because it will show up any sections that do not work well, giving you the chance to put them right before trying to find a publisher.

Q. *I've written a two-act play for the stage and would like to try to sell it. Where should I send it?*

A. The largest publisher of plays is Samuel French Ltd of London. Send them a synopsis and a sample scene rather than the entire script. If they like what they see, they'll ask for the complete play.

Q. *Are there any associations to which it would be useful for an aspiring dramatist to belong?*

A. There is the New Playwrights Trust, which unpublished playwrights may join. The major association is The Writers' Guild of Great Britain, which represents professional writers including playwrights and screenwriters. You may be eligible for temporary membership (see Useful Addresses, pp. 196, 197).

Radio Drama

Q. *I'm writing a half-hour play for radio. How do I know if I've got it to the correct length?*

A. The only reliable method of assessing length is to act it out and time it, allowing for all the 'business' (for example, shutting and opening doors as actors exit and enter rooms). Bear in mind that its duration will be slightly less than half an hour because of announcements of title, names of actors and so on.

Q. *Could you advise on the correct way to set out a radio play script?*

A. Speeches are numbered on each page. They are typed in single spacing with a double space between each one. Never indicate how you think an actor should speak the lines unless it is vital to the play, for example, if you want a character to speak in sarcastic tones. Well-written dialogue should be capable of standing alone.

The names of the characters should be separated from the dialogue and written in full each time so that it is clear who is speaking. The following is a short example of how a script should be set out:

(EXTERIOR, SOUNDS OF A LOUD EXPLOSION
FOLLOWED BY SCREAMS AND RUNNING
FOOTSTEPS)

1. MARTHA: Mother! Mother, where are you? I can't

see you. I can't see anything.

2. HILDA *(In faint voice from a distance):*
   I'm in here. The door's stuck. I can't –
   I can't open it.

Q. *In a radio play, do you have to consider other elements apart from dialogue?*

A. Sound effects (SFX), silence, pauses and music are integral elements of writing for radio. These should be underlined, typed in capitals and separated from dialogue. The BBC's notes on writing for radio, *Writing Plays for Radio – BBC Radio Drama*, which have recently been updated, include a specimen layout of a radio play script. They are available on request (don't forget to enclose a stamped, self-addressed envelope) from: The Chief Producer, Plays, BBC Radio Drama, Broadcasting House, London W1A 1AA. The BBC also has sample pages of scripts available if you send a stamped, self-addressed envelope to the Drama Department, BBC, Broadcasting House, London W1A 1AA.

Q. *How do you scene-set in a radio play?*

A. The usual way is to signpost at the end of one scene that it is about to move to another location or even time. For example, if one of your characters was about to go to Paris, you might have another saying: 'Wish I was coming with you, John. I've always wanted to visit Gay Paree.' The listener is then mentally prepared for the following scene to take place in the French capital.

Q. *How do I go about getting a play accepted for radio?*

A. There are three routes to take. One is to submit it to The Chief Producer for Single Plays at the BBC, London. The second, worth trying if your play has a regional flavour, is to submit it to the relevant Radio

Production Centre: Northern Ireland (Belfast), Wales (Cardiff), Scotland (Edinburgh), the Midlands (Birmingham) or the North of England (Manchester). (Full addresses are given in the BBC's notes on radio drama.) The third, and possibly the best, route is to listen regularly and then to send your play to an individual drama producer in London who seems to favour plays of a similar type to yours and whose work you admire.

Yet another way in is to enter any radio play competitions available. Currently, there are First Bite, for which entrants must be thirty or under, and the Alfred Bradley Bursary Award for plays with a Northern 'flavour'.

Following the dismantling of the script department at the BBC some time ago, it has become increasingly difficult to break in with a first play for radio but, as always, it is a question of perseverance. And it goes without saying that you should listen regularly and know all the current drama slots, their length, who has produced them and from which regional studio they were broadcast.

Q. *I have an idea for a series for radio. Whom, at the BBC, should I send it to?*

A. Anyone with an idea for either a series or a serial should send a detailed outline to the Chief Producer for Series and Serials at the BBC, London.

Q. *My ambition is to write radio drama and I listen to as many broadcast plays as possible. But is there any other way I can study the kind of play the BBC is looking for?*

A. Listening to what is currently being broadcast is undoubtedly the best way but, from time to time, anthologies of either award-winning plays or what are considered to be the best plays broadcast are published.

100

Methuen Drama and BBC Publications publish collections of The Giles Cooper Award-winning plays, the most recent being *Best Radio Plays 1991* which, although out of print, would be worth studying.

Q. *I have an idea for a radio play. Can I submit a synopsis only, in the first instance?*

A. No. You must submit the entire play but you should also include a synopsis, together with a full cast list and brief notes on the main characters.

Television Drama

Q. *I've no previous experience of writing drama but would like to try writing for television. What is the best route to take?*

A. Become known first through radio drama. From time to time, new writers for the soaps are sought through advertisements placed in the national press. There is heavy competition for these vacancies but someone has to fill them so it is always worthwhile responding. Occasionally, there are drama competitions which offer another possible way of breaking into this field.

Q. *Are there any openings for short sketches for either TV or radio?*

A. Many TV and radio comedians are constantly on the look-out for new material. If you think you can write for a particular comedian, study his/her performances so that you get a feel for the kind of material they use, write one or two pieces specifically for them and send them directly to them. If possible, find out who their agent is but, if you can't, write to them c/o the radio or television programme in which they regularly appear.

Q. *Are all writers for radio and TV paid at the same rate?*

A. No. There is usually a sliding scale and new writers will be paid at the lowest rate, moving up the scale as they become better known.

Q. *I've had two novels published and now would like to try writing for television. How can I break in?*

A. Whilst the one-off television play has been something of a rarity in recent years, and those which have appeared have been by well-known names, there is now a slight but discernible shift towards encouraging new writers in this field. To this end, the Teddington Arts Performance Showcase (TAPS), sponsored by Panasonic Broadcast and Teddington Studios, was launched in 1993 to provide the opportunity for exposure of aspiring TV dramatists' work to producers and directors. However, certain criteria must be fulfilled in order to be considered for this.

- Writers must be British.
- Writers must obtain and complete a submission form, before sending in a script (see Useful Addresses, p. 197). Unsolicited scripts will be returned unread.
- Complete scripts only must be submitted, of whatever length.
- A synopsis/outline of the play must be included
- Scripts should be set out in correct format for TV drama.

Four elements are specifically looked for:

- Originality of storyline.
- Effective dialogue.
- Dramatic structure.
- Knowledge of the market (that is, of current TV drama slots).

TAPS is only looking for professional writers who have already achieved success in the field of radio or stage drama or fiction writing and who want to extend their horizons to TV drama. But they must not have had more than two hours of drama on television.

Q. *What is the correct way to set out a script for television?*

A. A TV script is always written on the right-hand side of the page only, as in the following example:

> MARY LOOKS AT JOHN IN ASTONISHMENT
>
> MARY: What on earth are you doing here? I thought you were still in Cornwall?
>
> JOHN: I'm supposed to be. But I couldn't stand it another day. So – here I am, darling.
>
> JOHN MOVES TOWARDS MARY, ARMS OUTSTRETCHED.
>
> MARY TURNS AWAY, CLEARLY ANNOYED

Film Scripts

Q. *I've written a play which I think would make an ideal film script, but I haven't any contacts in the film world. How should I go about interesting someone in it?*

A. Your chances are very slim unless you are already an established writer. Assuming this is not so, and also that you have done your homework and are familiar with the work of individual producers and directors, you could write to one or more of them with a brief outline of your script and ask if they would be willing to read it. But be prepared for rejection.

Q. *My ambitions lie in the field of film and television. What chance is there for a new writer with a script suitable for either medium?*

A. 'Very little' is the honest answer. But if your script really is superb and you are prepared to keep trying, it is always possible that you might succeed. You could send a brief outline of the story to any or all of the agents who specialise in film and TV (see *The Writers' and Artists' Year Book* or *The Writer's Handbook*). Better still, of course, would be a personal introduction to someone in the industry.

POETRY

Q. *Are there any markets for poetry?*

A. They are few and far between, consisting mostly of small-circulation magazines. However, by dint of careful market study, it is possible to find occasional openings for poems relevant to a particular magazine. For instance, those concentrating on country living might take the odd one with a countryside angle. Women's magazines, too, take the occasional poem, particularly humorous verse.

There are a number of small poetry and/or literary magazines which use them. The Poetry Society or any local poetry group to which you might belong should be able to keep you informed about these. There are also several poetry competitions held annually, some of which subsequently publish anthologies. Radio, both local and national, sometimes broadcasts poetry.

The Association of Little Presses issues *Poetry and Little Press Information*, which should contain up-to-date information on possible markets (see Useful Addresses, p. 195).

Q. *What is the difference between blank verse and free verse?*

A. Blank verse is unrhymed five-foot iambic while free verse is not metric and may or may not be rhymed.

Q. *Should I send one poem only to a publication?*

A. Often, it pays to send several – up to six – at a time.

Q. *I have a large collection of poems written over the past ten years. I'd like to get them published in one volume. Is a publisher likely to be interested as I am unknown in the field?*

A. If you are completely unknown, it is highly unlikely that any bona fide publisher would consider your work.

Q. *I appreciate I'm not likely to find a publisher for my poetry but are there any other ways of producing it in the form of an anthology?*

A. Apart from self-publishing, you could approach your regional Arts Council. Sometimes, if you have a reputation as a local poet, they are able to subsidise the publication of a small volume of work.

Q. *Have you any advice to offer a completely unknown writer trying to establish himself and build up a reputation as a poet?*

A. Apart from trying to sell the occasional poem in whatever markets are available, enter every available competition, especially the major national ones. If you start to win prizes or receive commendations for your poetry, you will begin to attract attention in this field.

Q. *Would it be helpful to belong to a poetry group, either local or national?*

A. Yes. Your local library should be able to tell you if there is a group near you – most large towns and cities will have one. You should also find it advantageous to join the Poetry Society (see Useful Addresses, p. 196).

Q. *I like writing what I would describe as doggerel of the humorous variety. Is there any sale for such?*

A. Not really, apart from, perhaps, in a magazine if it is apt for a particular one.

SUMMING UP

You have considered the various genres of fiction writing and decided which you want to tackle, in the first instance. You may even have completed a piece of fiction, perhaps a short story, or are part way through a novel, but feel it is not quite right. At this point, it might help to take a look at some of the fiction techniques which are needed if you are to produce a successful story.

Fiction Techniques

In this section, we will examine some of those techniques which every successful writer of fiction uses. Often, it is just a question of understanding some of the tricks of the writer's trade which will bring that elusive success your way. We will also look at structure and plot and consider how much or how little planning is necessary before actually starting to write.

By the end of this part of the book, you should be ready to put into practice everything you have learned so far.

STRUCTURE

Q. *Why is the beginning of a novel considered to be more important than the rest?*

A. Because if the reader's interest is not captured immediately, he is likely to turn to something else. Because publishers receive such a vast number of manuscripts every week, it is vital for the new novelist to attract the attention of the editor or publisher's reader straight away. Therefore, unless the first three pages, at most, make him/her want to read on, the chances are he will give the rest of the book only a cursory glance – or read no further.

Q. *I realise my novel is too short and I have to pad it out. How should I do this?*

A. For a start, *never* pad: you should expand – which is not the same thing at all. There are various ways of doing this and, provided your novel has a strong enough plot or storyline, it should not be too difficult. You could bring in one or two more characters. You might introduce a sub-plot, though this must become an integral part of the main story and not merely tacked on to add extra wordage. And you can add incident as long as it is relevant. You will have to rewrite your book completely, of course – there is no short cut.

PLOT

Q. *How would you define plot?*

A. There are various ways of defining plot but a simple one would be: a causally related sequence of steadily worsening events, leading to the climax, by which point the life of the main character(s) is irrevocably changed.

Note the term 'steadily worsening'. If things improve for the character(s) within a story without more crises arising, there will be no incentive to make the reader want to continue turning the pages: in effect, the story will have ended.

Q. *What is meant by the climax of a story?*

A. This is the highest, most dramatic point in a work of fiction, whether it be novel, short story or play. It is sometimes known as the 'blackest moment' or the 'obligatory scene'. A story without a climax will sag like a soufflé when the oven door is opened too soon, the result being a flop. It is the logical, inevitable result of the build-up of successive crises or complications which will be quickly followed by the resolution or dénouement and satisfactory ending.

Ending the story before the climax is reached is a common mistake of tyro writers and is one to be aware of if they are to succeed. Think of the shoot-out in the famous Western film *High Noon*. It is the inevitable result of everything that has gone before. The sheriff knows that both his life and his love are at stake if he takes up his gun and does battle, but believes he has no choice. If he simply decided to take the easy way out and walked away, the audience would be utterly dissatisfied with the ending. As it is, the final shoot-out (the climax) provides the tensest moment in the story; the sheriff wins and his bride realises he had no real choice but to fight an evil man, to the death if need be. Result: a satisfactory ending and, in this case, also a happy one.

Q. *What is meant by 'storyline'?*

A This is another way of saying plot. It should be possible to describe the storyline in a few sentences. For example, it is about a young woman whose husband has been killed in a car crash. While coming to terms with her loss, she finds she rather likes having her independence. She uses the insurance money to start up a small business, falls in love, then realises, just in time, that marrying again would be a retrograde step. She will be Charles's lover but not his wife. Her new-found freedom and independence are too valuable to lose.

PLANNING

Q. *How much time should you spend planning a novel before starting to write?*

A. This varies from author to author and depends on personal preference. Some spend considerable time on the planning, while others do very little, preferring to let the storyline develop as they write, and saying they couldn't continue without the element of finding out for themselves what happens next. However, the majority probably do a fair amount before starting on the actual writing. Charles Dickens, for instance, once wrote to his friend Wilkie Collins: 'You don't have the jolter-headedness of the amateur writer who thinks he can do it off the cuff.' A well-known modern writer, Iris Murdoch, plans in great detail, writing thousands of words outlining her stories before starting on the book proper.

Another novelist said that she knows the beginning and the end and a few ports of call in between. Phyllis A. Whitney, a highly successful American writer of romantic suspense, describes in her excellent *Guide to Fiction Writing* her own method of planning, which helps her whenever she finds her plot bogged down during the writing.

In the end, each writer needs to discover what is their own best working method but probably somewhere between the two extremes is the norm.

Q. *How much information should be given in the first chapter of a novel?*

A. The readers should be introduced to the main character and learn where the novel is set and what period, that is, whether it is contemporary or set back in time or in the future. They must also know what the main thrust of the story will be (what is the main character's driving force – to find a lost child, recover an old home/business, find a murderer, and so on); what its tone is (is it humorous, a whodunnit, a horror story, a light romance, a poignant love story?). The 'point of change' which sets the story in motion must also be there.

CHARACTERS MAKE YOUR STORY

Q. *Is it always necessary to have a main character or protagonist in a novel?*

A. There must always be a protagonist on whom readers can focus, even in a novel in which there may be several major characters. By convention, it is usually the first one to be mentioned, either in a novel or in a short story. Protagonist literally means 'the leading character in a play'.

Q. *My novel was recently rejected by a publisher who said the characters lacked believable motivation. What does that mean?*

A. Motivation is of vital importance if a character's actions are to be believable. Good fiction is always character-driven. Otherwise, no matter how ingenious your plot, readers will soon realise that you are manipulating the characters to fit your plot, rather than the plot resulting from the characters' desires and drives. Remember the dictum: characters make your story. If your plot is character-driven, your novel will never be rejected because of poor motivation.

Q. *How do I go about creating believable characters?*

A. Many successful novelists advise writing a mini-biography for each important character. In this way, they are able to get to know them in depth, their physical, mental and emotional characteristics, their foibles, likes and dislikes, hobbies, careers, friends, families and so on.

Remember that a pronounced physical trait is likely to have an effect on your character's life. For instance, a deformity, a disability, or even being extremely tall or short, would affect how they think, act and react. Similarly, their background, childhood and their past generally, will all influence the present and, thus, what is happening at the time of your story. So the more you know about your characters, the more convincing they will become to your readers and the less like cardboard cut-outs.

Q. *What would happen if I inadvertently gave a character in my novel the name of an actual living person?*

A. Probably nothing. The danger would lie in portraying such a character in a bad light and making him readily identifiable with a living person (that is, giving him the same profession or putting him in a similar situation), laying yourself open to a libel suit. So far as is practicable, it is sensible to make sure your characters cannot be mistaken for real people.

Q. *I've been told the hero in my romantic novel is a stereotypical character? What does this mean?*

A. It is another way of saying that your hero is a cardboard cut-out rather than one who comes over as a believable, real-life character made of flesh and blood. To overcome this weakness, try giving him an unusual hobby or career or physical trait.

Know everything about your main characters so they become as real to you as your closest friend. Avoid cliché descriptions such as dark, tangled locks, sapphire/emerald/china-blue eyes, heart-shaped lips. Don't make your heroes dark, brooding Heathcliff clones. Give both hero and heroine a flaw or two, though none so terrible that no one could possibly fall in love with them. Remember that a caring heart lay beneath Mr Darcy's proud exterior.

Q. *I want to introduce into my novel characters whose experiences and background are totally different from my own. Is this something too difficult to attempt?*

A. Not necessarily – in the sense that most people will have experienced most of the *emotions* human beings are heir to. However, if you are giving your characters careers or a particular background with which you are not personally familiar, you will have to do considerable research, including talking to people who have this knowledge, to ensure its authenticity. You would also be wise, after your novel is finished, to get someone with this intimate knowledge to read it and check you have not made any glaring errors.

The kind of character it might be best to avoid creating, as a new writer, is one from a different culture from your own. But, if you have a strong desire to depict characters from a background alien to your own, there is no reason why you should not do so provided you undertake sufficient research. Indeed, a hugely successful novel, *Nile*, set in Egypt against an Islamic cultural background, was written by an American woman, Laurie Devine. She had no personal experience of the incidents and events which affected her Egyptian peasant heroine, who was so vividly portrayed that it was difficult to believe she had not. On the other hand, Charles Dickens based David Copperfield on himself as a boy and Harper Lee (*To Kill a Mockingbird*) knew what it was like to be a small child in a small Southern town in America.

VIEWPOINT

Q. *What are the viewpoints to consider in fiction-writing?*

A. In effect, there are three:

- First-person
- Third-person
- Omniscient

With the first person, it is usually the main character

who is telling the story. Occasionally, however, the first-person narrator may be a minor character, relating events concerning and involving someone else.

Telling a story in the third person is the most common method in both the novel and the short story. In a novel it allows events to be seen through the eyes of more than one character. Known as multiple viewpoint, it offers the author greater freedom but needs to be exercised judiciously. As Allan Massie explained in an article in the *Daily Telegraph* some years ago, 'The writer is always tempted to dissipate the interest; he is then corrupted by his freedom, and the intensity achieved by a consistent point of view is out of reach.' He went on to quote Graham Greene, who said, 'This happens, sometimes with writers I'd call "secondary" – and invariably with bad writers.'

The word 'omniscient' literally means 'all-seeing' and this point of view is often known as 'the god's-eye view'. It will be used to scene-set in a novel but, because of its necessarily detached nature, is rarely used in the short story.

Q.   *Are there any advantages to writing in the first person?*

A.   Graham Greene suggested that it offers an obvious technical advantage because it insures against any temptation to deviate.

It also helps create immediacy, making it easier for readers to believe they are hearing about something which really happened to the narrator (the 'I' of the story), thus drawing them more deeply into the story. Stories written for radio often benefit from choosing this viewpoint.

Q.   *Are there any advantages in sticking to a single viewpoint throughout a novel?*

A.   No, it is solely a question of personal preference. In fact, relating the story through the eyes of several characters gives greater scope to explore many facets of the story and to introduce sub-plots, adding to the complexity and resulting in a richer texture. But beware of constantly switching viewpoint, which can become irritating.

Q. *I'm planning my first novel. I've been considering writing it in the first person singular but what restrictions would that impose?*

A. If you begin in the first person, you would have to use it throughout. (There have been a few notable exceptions to this but, for an inexperienced writer, it would be unwise to attempt it.) The main restriction is that the reader can know only what the 'I' knows, hears or sees, though there are ways to overcome this such as the narrator observing another's expression or body language and guessing what they are thinking. The 'I' can also imagine what is happening somewhere else, thus suggesting to the reader that this is so.

In certain genres such as romantic-suspense and gothic novels, the advantage of immediacy outweighs such restrictions and it has become a convention to tell the story in this way, from classics such as Charlotte Brontë's *Jane Eyre* and Daphne du Maurier's *Rebecca* to modern novels by such writers as Mary Stewart and Phyllis A. Whitney.

Q. *How do you decide which viewpoint to use when starting a novel?*

A. It is often a question of trial and error. Many writers say that they sometimes find a story doesn't 'gel' when they start writing in, say, the first person and they have to change to the third person before it begins to work, or vice versa.

Q. *Why is it considered wrong to change viewpoint in a short story?*

A. Because of its brevity and tight structure, there is not much time or space in which to build up the necessary emotion towards the character whose story is unfolding. Therefore, it is wise not to dissipate that emotional energy.

Q. *Although I understand the reasons for staying with one viewpoint in a short story, I find I slip into another without realising it. How can I overcome this problem?*

A. This is a common difficulty for many new writers. If you write in the first person, it should make it almost impossible to stray, because if you then wish to change to the third person, it will be relatively easy to go through the story, when finished, and change the 'I' to 'he' or 'she'.

Q. *How do I decide from which character's viewpoint to tell a story?*

A. Choose the character from whom you can wrest the most emotion. It is possible to write from the viewpoint of any of the characters involved and you need to consider which one you most empathise with. For instance, if the plot revolved round a young couple wishing to emigrate, taking with them their small son and leaving behind a widowed grandparent, a writer who was an older woman would probably see the story from the latter's point of view rather from that of the young mother or father.

Q. *What is meant by the term 'a story within a frame'?*

A. If a short story is narrated in the first person singular by a minor character who is an onlooker, rather than by the main character who is actively involved, the result may be what is often known as a 'story within a frame'.

This is nowadays considered a somewhat old-fashioned stylistic device, which is best avoided.

DIALOGUE

Q. *Could you explain about dialogue. What are its functions in fiction?*

A. A large percentage of dialogue as compared with narrative is generally preferred today, particularly in popular, commercial fiction, because it increases the pace of a novel. It should be included only if it fulfils a specific function, of which there are basically three:

- To move the story/plot forward.
- To help characterise.
- To provide necessary information (that is, information which the reader needs to have in order to understand what is happening).

Social chit-chat or small-talk has no part in fiction. For instance, if it is important for the reader to know that it has been raining heavily, you need not have one character remark on this to another *unless they are both involved in the subsequent action of the story*. Otherwise, it is enough to have one character thinking about the bad weather.

If one character must find out something about another in order to force him into action, this would be a good place to use dialogue. Perhaps one overhears the other or is taken into another's confidence.

'I hear Joe's being sent overseas, next week,' Philip remarked casually.

'I don't believe it,' Tony snapped. 'He would have told me if it was true. I had a drink with him yesterday evening.'

That short snatch of conversation suggests that Tony will now seek out Joe to find out if it really is true and, if so, will react in some way. We also learn that, if Joe is actually leaving, it is going to have an impact on Tony and that Philip is in a better position to hear such things. Thus, it fulfilled all three requirements at the same time.

Q. *Does every piece of dialogue have to be followed by 'said' or other speech tag?*

A. No. In fact, as long as it is clear who is speaking, it tends to sharpen the style if you cut out unnecessary speech tags. For example, following a speech with a piece of action will indicate who has spoken:

> 'I'm not going, and that's that.' John slammed his fist on the table.

There is no need to add 'John said' as it is obvious John has just spoken.

FLASHBACK

Q. *Is it necessary to have flashbacks in a work of fiction?*

A. Invariably, yes. It is the vehicle for understanding motivation, for explaining *why* a character is acting in a particular way – that is, what emotion is driving him. It is this *why* which is so important in fiction-writing, though flashbacks will necessarily be much briefer in a short story than in a novel.

Nancy Hale in *The Realities of Fiction* says: 'If he [the writer] fails to establish a strong and acceptable motive, he can save his best writing and his keenest observations; they will not help ... If strong enough motives are provided, rooted in the hearts and nerves of the characters, action will automatically follow.' And, without using flashback for this purpose, it would be necessary

118

to 'tell' in straight narrative rather than 'show' in a scene the reasons for the current action.

SHOW, DON'T TELL

Q. *I've been told it is important, in a work of fiction, to show and not tell. Can you explain what that means?*

A. This simply means making a scene of any important incident in a story so that the reader can visualise it as if it were taking place on a stage in front of him. For example, suppose two of your characters were chatting together when a masked man burst into the room, wielding a gun. Clearly, this would be a dramatic scene in the study and, as such, should be shown *happening*, not merely related in straight narrative. Thus, it might be written like this:

> John's mouth dropped open in disbelief as the door burst open. 'What the hell— ' he began, only to be interrupted by Martha's hysterical scream as she flung herself into his arms. The next few seconds seemed to him like something out of a horror film. The burly, balaclava-clad man waved a gun menacingly at them. In guttural tones, he ordered, 'Get on the floor, both of you – or you'll get this!' The gun swung purposefully in their direction.
>
> 'It's all right, Martha,' John murmured, trying to calm his sister. 'Do as he says and I'm sure he won't harm us.' But Martha was past all reasoning and continued to utter panic-stricken shrieks. John was forced to grab her and push her to the ground. Shielding her trembling body with his own, he managed to glance sideways and upwards. Dark eyes gleamed malevolently out of black, roughly-cut holes. John's stomach gave a violent lurch and he felt a cold sweat break out across his brow.

There is no need to *tell* the reader that John is desperately afraid or that he is trying to protect his sister – we have *seen* it.

PACE

Q.   *I've been told my novel lacks pace. What does that mean?*

A.   The most likely meaning is that it is too slow-moving, that there is not enough action. Take a good, hard look at it and ask yourself if you have spent too long describing the scenery, perhaps. Maybe there is too much narrative compared with dialogue? Plenty of dialogue (provided it fulfils one of its functions and is not merely social chit-chat), increases a story's pace.

Raymond Chandler's advice to authors, for when a story begins to flag, was to bring in a man with a gun. In other words, make something happen, which will increase the pace.

However, pace should be varied to include some slower, more reflective passages so that the reader can catch his breath, metaphorically. Otherwise, the story would rush onwards like an express train, leaving him feeling breathless. But in commercial fiction, it is generally true that if you aim for a cracking pace you won't go far wrong.

CONFLICT

Q.   *I've been told my stories lack conflict. What does this mean and why is conflict necessary?*

A.   There is a truism, 'no conflict, no story'. Without it, there will be no tension or suspense and little to make the reader want to keep turning the pages. The problem, especially for new writers, seems to lie in defining the word itself. It does not mean solely violence, either physical or verbal, but refers to any type of confrontational situation. There are two types of conflict, internal and external, which are sub-divided into three areas:

1. Man against man (external)
2. Man against himself (internal)
3. Man against nature (external).

Man against Man

This might be two people disagreeing over something of considerable importance to one of them. A teenage daughter wanting to stay out late, for instance, and her father refusing permission. Or it might be two gunslingers battling for supremacy.

Man against Himself

This will be an inner battle against conscience or some strong emotion such as love, guilt, fear, shame and so on.

Man against Nature

Here your character could be struggling against a storm or flood or fierce desert heat, perhaps as a result of a plane crash or similar.

However you use it, conflict *must* be there if you hope to write a successful piece of fiction.

Q. *What is meant by lack of tension?*

A. The effect of no tension in a story is that the reader will have no incentive to continue to turn the pages: the 'what happens next?' element is missing.

Q. *How can I increase the tension in my story?*

A. By combining internal and external conflict in any one scene in a story, the tension (and suspense) will be considerably increased. For instance, in man against nature, a character might be faced not only with having to cross a river in flood but also with the inner battle against his fear of water.

Bridging Scenes

Q. *What are bridging, or transitional, scenes and how important are they?*

A. They are necessary to inform the reader that the action of a story has moved from one place to another or from one time to another. This can be effected by a short scene, by a single sentence or by a break in the text with an asterisk or row of asterisks between the text sections.

An example of the first technique would be: 'When Simon awoke the next morning, he found that the river had gone down to its normal level and he was able to cross to the other side.' The story can then continue on the other side of the river, leaving the reader in no doubt about where Simon is. Or you could say simply, 'Next morning ...'

Summing Up

In the foregoing four sections, we have looked at the many and various elements involved in the complex business of writing and are ready to proceed to the next step. You will now appreciate the truth of what Hippocrates said more than two thousand years ago: 'The life so short, the craft so long to learn.' And writing *is* a craft. However much natural talent you have, it is still necessary to learn how to employ certain techniques and to study the craftsmanship of other writers to help you on the road to success. You are now ready to take the next important step towards becoming a writer.

The Next Step

You are ready to send your work out to an editor or publisher or even to try to find an agent willing to handle it for you. But how do you go about it?

First, you must study the market at which you are aiming and how to tackle it in order to increase your chances of success. You must also realise the importance of revision in order to make your work as good as you possibly can. And, inevitably, you will have to face having your work rejected.

This vast, new and exciting world has a language all of its own, which you need to learn. You will be introduced to all these issues in the following section, which will take you further along your chosen path.

REVISION

Q. *I find that once I've written a story I don't want to go over it again. How important is it to revise?*

A. Revision of any piece of writing is a vital part of the entire process. Most best-selling authors say they rewrite several times before they feel happy with their book – for instance, Jeffrey Archer says that he wrote seventeen drafts of *As the Crow Flies*. Ernest Hemingway rewrote the last page of *A Farewell to Arms* no fewer than thirty-nine times before he was satisfied with it. And each day he re-read and edited the previous day's work before continuing, reckoning that, in total, he probably wrote the book several hundred times.

If you send an editor or publisher work which gives the impression of having been written quickly and without care, you are far more likely to have it rejected. As the Latin poet Horace said nearly two thousand years ago, 'Often must you turn your stylus to erase.' Wise words, if you hope to produce something worth a second reading.

Q. *What sort of things should I be looking for when revising?*

A. There are a number of things which frequently need to be carefully checked, the commonest being spelling and punctuation. If you know you have a weakness here, don't trust to luck but check with a dictionary and grammar book. Alternatively, ask someone whose English you know is impeccable to look it over for you before you send your work out.

Repetition is something else that should not be overlooked when revising. Cutting and pruning invariably improve one's writing. Check how many times you have used the same word on a single page and see where it could be eliminated or exchanged for a synonym.

See if you can reduce the number of adverbs and adjectives used, keeping only those which produce the strongest effect. Be ruthless in taking out any so-called 'purple passages', thus helping to keep your style simple and more effective.

Have you included anything which might be considered padding? If so, cut it out. Are you guilty of qualifying words which are unqualifiable (fairly unique; completely dead)? It's easily done but demonstrates slack writing. Are you sure the unfamiliar word you've used means what you intend?

Finally, read it through, out loud if possible, to ensure its rhythm is smooth and pleasing, bearing in mind the truism 'Write for the ear, not for the eye'.

If you take the time to revise your work, you'll stand a better chance of acceptance.

Q. *Is there any single piece of advice about revision which might help improve my chances of success?*

A. The simplest and possibly the best piece of advice is to put away whatever you've written for several weeks or for as long as is practicable. Then take it out and reread critically and objectively to see if it can be improved at all before submission to an editor or publisher. After this time-lapse, faults often appear which were not apparent before.

Q. *I've just had an article returned by a national magazine editor, who said she liked the idea, but ... She wants me to rewrite it along the lines she's suggested. However, I feel that, if I did this, it would no longer be my own piece. What would you advise?*

A. First of all, how important is it to you to make a sale? If you're in the early stages of your writing career, getting your byline known could be very important. Secondly, the fact that the editor was sufficiently interested in your article suggests that you'd done part of your market study correctly, having found a subject suitable for the magazine, but you hadn't written it up to its requirements.

You would be wise to swallow your pride (a professional writer doesn't have this kind of pride), contact the editor immediately and agree to the suggested rewrite. Bear in mind that it is her job to know in what form material should be presented for her particular magazine. However, if, after careful consideration, you still feel strongly that it would go against your principles, write a polite, diplomatic letter withdrawing it. But weigh against that the fact that that editor may never bother to make such a suggestion again, if you have a 'near miss' in the future.

Q. *Can too much rewriting spoil a story?*

A. That rather depends on what is meant by too much. As already pointed out, most successful authors do a good deal of rewriting. They prune and polish their work until they feel it is as near perfect as they can make it. Almost invariably, cutting, and thus tightening, a piece of prose will improve it – though you don't want to destroy its life. Try to strike a balance between improving style and structure and keeping your writing's freshness and originality. The best test is to put it away for a few weeks at least, then take a long, hard, objective look at it before doing whatever rewriting you then feel will improve it. After that, if you continue to tinker with it, it might start to lose something of its spontaneity.

MARKET STUDY

Q. *I understand the need to keep studying the market before submitting work but it becomes expensive if one continually has to buy magazines. Can you suggest any way round this?*

A. When you are starting to write, and until you have a clear idea of the type of market at which you want to aim, you will need to look at as many different publications as possible. This, of course, does become expensive if you have to buy them all, but ask friends and family to let you see copies of any they take, which will reduce the initial cost. Take advantage of places which put out magazines for people whiling away time, such as doctors' and dentists' waiting-rooms and hair-dressers. Spend the occasional half-hour browsing along magazine racks at the larger newsagents and don't forget that your local public library's reference section will have a selection.

Once you have invested some time in this first step, you will be in a position to focus on those specific publications for which you would like to write and where you feel you stand some chance of success. At that point, you will need to analyse several current issues (at least three and preferably more). If you have to purchase them, it should prove money well spent because it will increase your chance of recouping what you have laid out.

Q. *How can I get hold of a particular newspaper or trade magazine which isn't readily available but which I want to study?*

A. You can write to the editor and ask for a copy, offering to pay for it. Explain that you are a freelance writer and wish to study it in the hope of being able to contribute. More than likely, you will receive a free copy of a recent issue.

Q. *Where can I find out about trade and specialist magazines?*

A. Many specialist magazines, such as those covering hobbies from stamp-collecting to water sports, are available through the larger outlets for magazines and books. Many are listed in *The Writer's Handbook* and *The Writers' and Artists' Year Book*. Another useful source is *1000 Markets for Freelance Writers* by Robert Palmer. For trade magazines with which you are not familiar, you can find details in *Willing's Press Guide* which should be available in the reference section of larger public libraries.

Q. *How do I find the right publisher for my book?*

A. By market research. Browse in bookshops and libraries to see who is currently publishing which type of book, be it fiction or non-fiction, and especially those in the same category as your own. Look at the most recent issue of *The Writer's Handbook* or *The Writers' and Artists' Year Book*, which will also give a general idea of individual requirements. Not until you have done this should you consider submitting your manuscript anywhere.

Q. *How do I analyse a market?*

A. First of all, make sure that whichever particular publication you are studying accepts unsolicited material. If not, then you will be wasting your time analysing it. Then obtain at least four current issues (looking at any which appeared a long time ago could be useless as editorial policies may have changed since then).

The next step is to study it in depth, listing everything you can possibly glean about it. What type of reader is it aimed at? Male or female; young, middle-aged or elderly; career women or stay-at-home housewives; socio-economic group; political stance, if any. The advertisements will give some strong clues.

What sort of subjects are covered? Hobbies, career-orientated, general interest, women/family-orientated? Are the articles mainly informative or light-hearted entertainment?

What style or tone of voice is used? Does the publication contain fiction as well as non-fiction and, if so, what is the ratio?

Do there appear to be any taboo subjects? Are any topics regularly covered by the same writer, suggesting they might be staff-written? If so, there will be little point in your trying to break in there. Also, look at the length of material. Are there some very short pieces which, in effect, are 'fillers' (50–350 words long)? Are most of them about one page in length (usually

800–1000 words)? Are some considerably longer, covering certain topics in greater detail? How many are illustrated with photographs or line drawings?

Next, read the fiction in it, not just for pleasure but to discover what sort of stories it contains. What age are the characters in the different stories? If the main character is often an older woman, that suggests the readers are female and probably over about fifty. If usually a young married woman with small children, you could safely assume that they are the main buyers of the magazine. Are most of the stories romantic or are some in the 'human interest' category? Do they sometimes involve children or animals? Do any of them have twist endings?

It is only when you have gleaned as much information as possible from analysing your chosen publication in depth that you should try to write for it.

Finally, make a careful note of the relevant editor – fiction or features – for the type of material you are interested in submitting, making sure you spell his or her name correctly. Then, when you are ready to send work in, you can address it to that editor.

Q.   *How do I analyse a short story?*

A.   Take a sheet of paper and make a list of the following questions:

- Who is the main character?
- What are the main character's age and socio-economic group?
- What viewpoint is used, first- or third-person? If the latter, does it change or remain the same throughout the story?
- What other characters appear in the story?
- What is the tone of the story? Is it tender, romantic, dramatic, spooky, frightening, exciting, human-interest, poignant? It should be clear from the beginning what this is.

- When are the events taking place? Now, back in time or in the future?
- What is the proportion of dialogue to narrative?
- What is the main character's problem or goal? This should be obvious in the first few paragraphs.
- What is the initial crisis that sets the story in motion?
- What are the subsequent crises with which the main character has to deal?
- What is the climax of the story – the 'blackest moment' for the main character?
- What is the story's resolution? Is it a satisfactory ending?

Then reread a story published in your target magazine, and see how the author has dealt with each question. Once you have stripped the story to its bare bones, you should have some idea of why it appealed to the editor and appeared in print. In other words, you should then know what made that particular story work. You can now begin to look at any of your own stories which have been rejected and see where they went wrong and if it is possible to rewrite them.

Q.   *How do I know if a magazine will consider unsolicited material?*

A.   Usually, it will state somewhere inside the cover if it does or not.

Q.   *How do I know which material is staff-written?*

A.   Study at least four, and preferably six, issues. If you find the same name appearing in each issue covering the same subject matter, you can be reasonably sure that it is written by a member of staff.

Q.   *Is there any way of finding out a magazine's requirements?*

A.   Many magazines produce tip-sheets or guidelines for contributors. Write to the editorial office (the address is normally inside the front cover), enclosing a stamped, self-addressed envelope. While guidelines are useful, they should only be an addition to your own study of individual markets. You should still read and analyse several issues before attempting to write for them.

FINDING A PUBLISHER

Q. *I've just finished the final draft of my first novel and want to find a publisher. Can I send it to more than one at once?*

A. This is known as multiple submission and is common practice in the USA. In the UK, also, there is no reason why you should not send out several copies simultaneously, provided you say so in your covering letter. It might even ensure that it is looked at more quickly in case more than one publishing house would want to buy it. But, remember, this applies only to novels, not to short stories.

Q. *Is it better to send a synopsis and two or three chapters to a publisher or agent rather than the complete book?*

A. Many publishers and agents prefer the former although a few would rather see the entire novel. Many, however, prefer a preliminary letter in which the story is outlined in a couple of short paragraphs. They should be able to tell from this whether it would be suitable for their lists.

Q. *I've finished an 80,000-word novel and want to find a publisher. However, I'm worried that it might be stolen by someone in the publisher's office and then submitted as their own work. Am I being neurotic about this or could it actually happen?*

A. The chances of such an occurrence are so remote that you should not worry about it. For one thing, the staff in a publishing house are unlikely to be writers themselves. For another, companies would soon go out of business if they were found to be publishing novels written by someone other than the author named on the book's jacket. Thirdly, don't forget that your work is automatically protected by copyright law from the moment it is written and, as you would have a copy of it, even if only on disk, you would be able to prove in a court of law that it belonged to you.

Concentrate on ensuring you have written as good a book as possible and put aside all worries about someone stealing it.

Q. *I want to send a publisher a synopsis of my novel and three chapters. Should I send the first chapter, one from the middle and, say the last?*

A. Most publishers prefer to see the first three chapters. None likes random chapters to be submitted as these will not enable them to tell if the story progresses in a smooth, logical sequence to the end. And *never* submit odd pages from the book.

Q. *I've just finished my first novel (a thriller) which is 40,000 words long. Can you give me any advice about how to get it published?*

A. At 40,000 words it is far too short to stand any chance of acceptance. It needs to be doubled in length before you consider submitting it to a publishing house.

Q. *What do publishers look for in a novel? I've submitted three, all without success.*

A. That is a difficult question as, to some extent at least, the answer must be subjective. Obviously, every publisher hopes to find a novel with the potential to become a best-seller, so it must be a 'good read'. It must have believable, well-drawn characters, an interesting setting and background and a gripping storyline which compels the reader to keep turning the pages. It must have the illusive quality 'immediacy' which makes the reader willingly suspend his disbelief. Modern commercial novels must also have pace. Publishers and editors often say they don't know exactly what they want until they see it but it has to be a story that is difficult to put down. It must also be not merely as good as but better than others which land on their desk.

Q. *How can I find out which publishers are looking for what type of book?*

A. Look in bookshops and libraries to see what is currently being published and by whom and write to individual publishers for an up-to-date catalogue and/or tip-sheet, if it is available. As always, enclose a stamped, self-addressed envelope.

Q. *I'm thinking of offering a collection of short stories to a publisher. Do I stand any chance of acceptance?*

A. As an unknown writer, very little. Collections of short stories are not popular today. Occasionally, a publisher will bring out an anthology by different writers but it is rarely a commercial success. The sad fact is that readers don't buy books of short stories in sufficient numbers to make them commercially viable. Perhaps every aspiring short-story writer should determine to buy such anthologies whenever they do appear.

PRESENTATION AND SUBMISSION

Typescript Presentation

Q. *What is the correct way to write numbers and dates in a manuscript?*

A. Numbers up to and including a hundred are normally written in full, for example: twenty-one. After that, in figures (for example, 101) up to one thousand, two thousand, one million and so on. Dates are usually written, for example, 16 May 1924; 21 October 1863.

Q. *Can I submit work typed on both sides of the paper in order to economise?*

A. Definitely not. Work must always be presented on one side of the paper only in double-spaced typing.

Q. *I have been given a large supply of typing paper of the old foolscap size. Can I use this to submit work for publication?*

A. If you feel you cannot afford to buy the normal A4 paper, no editor or publisher is likely to reject a really good story because it is submitted on foolscap. However, it would make sense to use this for your own copies and submit work on the normal A4 to create a professional impression.

Q. *How do I indicate I want a word in italics?*

A. The accepted method is to underline any words or phrases which you want to appear in italics.

Q. *My word processor has a facility for full justification. Should I use this on my manuscript?*

A. No. Most publishers and editors do not like work to be fully justified (that is, making the right-hand margin symmetrical).

Q. *What is the correct way to number the pages in a novel?*

A. Always number the pages consecutively throughout any manuscript. Never number the pages of chapters separately.

Q. *I've heard that editors are suspicious of work which is submitted without alterations and corrections to the manuscript. Is this true?*

A. This is nonsense. With the advent and popular use of the word processor, perfect-looking manuscripts could not be easier to produce and, of course, are much easier to read. Ignore such ridiculous statements.

Q. *Do editors and publishers prefer or dislike any particular typefaces?*

A. All editors and publishers want a clear, straightforward typeface. They do not like fancy typefaces or one which is too large. If you stick to Times roman in 10-, 11- or 12-point, you won't go far wrong.

Submission of Work

Q. *I know I'm weak on grammar and spelling. Would an editor make any corrections if they liked my work?*

A. Submitting work full of grammatical errors not only demonstrates a lack of professionalism but suggests you do not consider your writing to be of much importance. Whilst a few mistakes might be forgiven and corrected by the sub-editor or copy-editor, too many might result in the speedy return of your manuscript. Always check thoroughly before sending it out, either with a good grammar book and dictionary or by getting someone to check it for you.

Q. *I've written several short stories aimed at a particular magazine. Should I send all of them at the same time?*

A. There is no law that says you cannot do this but, generally speaking, it is not a wise practice. Some editors seem to have an aversion to accepting more than one story at a time from the same author. Submit one and wait a few weeks; then, if it is not returned, send another. If it is rejected, try a second one right away.

If you submit your stories in fairly quick succession, the editor will notice your name and realise you are determined to break in. If you show promise, even if your work is not yet up to standard, the chances are you will eventually get a letter of encouragement, perhaps with helpful suggestions. If you send them all off in one batch this isn't likely, and if they come back together you might feel more despondent than if it happened over a period of several weeks or months.

Q.   *What is a cover sheet and what information should it contain?*

A.   The cover sheet is the front page of your manuscript giving all relevant details such as title of the piece, your name, address and so on, as shown in the following illustration:

The Waterohed

by

Mary Jones

A short story submitted by:
Mary Jones
Jeyes Farm
Bradbury
LE32 XYZ

Tel: Bradbury (01234) 123456

Length: Approx. 2100 words

First British Serial Rights Offered
24 August 1995

Q. *When submitting a novel, should I either paper-clip chapters separately or secure all the pages of the manuscript in a binder of some kind?*

A. Neither. The preferred method for submitting a full-length manuscript is to put a rubber-band around its loose pages and place in either an empty typing paper cardboard box or a reinforced envelope. Editors dislike having to remove clips or binding of any kind in order to extract a few pages to read at any one time.

Q. *I've been told to write First British Serial Rights at the bottom of my short story manuscripts before sending them to a magazine. What do these words mean?*

A. This is the accepted way of stating that you are only offering that particular publication the opportunity to print that story for the first time in Britain. It is another way of saying that you are not offering all rights and are retaining your copyright. This also applies to feature articles, though not to full-length works of any description. Very occasionally, especially with articles, you might wish to offer exactly the same piece to another publication in Britain. In that case, you must then offer Second British Serial Rights and you should also inform the editor where it first appeared.

Q. *Should the manuscript of a play for radio or television be submitted in loose-leaf form, the same as if it were a novel?*

A. No. This is the one form of writing where producers prefer the pages of the manuscript to be bound together and presented in a neat, clearly labelled cover.

Q. *I don't wish to use my real name on my writing so how should I let an editor know I want a pen-name to appear when it is published?*

A. On the cover sheet, type the name of your piece then, below, in place of your real name, put your pen-name, for example, Mary Bloggs. Below that, give your own name and address as shown. This will ensure that, when the story appears in print, your pen-name will be shown but your payment cheque will be made out in your own name.

Q. *As I use a word processor, is it acceptable to submit my novel on disk?*

A. In the first instance, a publisher will want to see the actual manuscript (or hard copy as it is also known). However, if accepted, provided your system is compatible with theirs, they will probably be glad of the disk. In your covering letter, therefore, you should say that it is available, and tell them what software you use.

It is becoming more and more common for books to be typeset from disk, rather than from hard copy, as it saves time and money.

Q. *Is it permissible to submit photocopies of an article or short story to a magazine?*

A. It is generally not advisable to do so, as the editor might suspect it had been sent to several other publications simultaneously.

Q. *I intend sending my novel to a number of publishers at the same time. Is there any reason why I should not send photocopies and keep the original myself?*

A. As long as you state in your covering letter that you have submitted your typescript to other publishers simultaneously, there should be no objection to a photocopy.

Q. *What size envelope should I use when submitting a shortish (consisting of a few pages) piece of writing such as a magazine article or short story?*

A.   Use an envelope which will allow a page of A4 paper to be folded in half. This would normally be $9 \times 6^1/_2$ inches. If you use a larger A4 envelope, thus not folding the pages, the sheets of paper are likely to be creased during transit.

Q.   *Should I send a covering letter with my manuscript?*

A.   It is largely a question of personal choice. If you are submitting a short story or article, it is not strictly necessary. A cover-sheet, containing all relevant information such as your name and address, length of piece and rights offered is sufficient. However, if you have previously had work accepted by that same publication or editor, it would make sense to write a short, personal letter reminding them of this, especially if it was some time ago. Similarly, if you are an expert on the particular subject of your article, it would be advantageous to inform the editor of this.

   If you are submitting a novel, of course, you must send a covering letter, giving any relevant information such as your personal knowledge of the background or setting used, if you have had short stories published in magazines and if you are working on another novel.

Q.   *I'm about to submit a proposal for a cookery book to a publisher and I have what I think is a good idea for illustrating the cover. Would it be wrong of me to suggest this?*

A.   Yes. This might be seen by the publisher as being presumptuous. In any case, if the book were accepted, the publisher would employ a professional artist to design the cover. The marketing department would probably also be involved to ensure the book's cover had the best possible eye-appeal. At that stage, though, you could let your editor know of your ideas.

Q.   *I've written a story for radio which I've put on to a cassette.*

Should I send the manuscript or would it be considered useful to send the cassette?

A. Send the manuscript only. The BBC will not consider recorded material, and if a story is accepted for broadcasting it will be read by a professional actor.

Q. *Would it be possible for me to read my own story on the air if it were accepted by the BBC?*

A. No, not unless you are also a professional actor with an Equity card.

Q. *When I send my manuscript to a publisher, whom should I address it to?*

A. Whenever possible, address it to an individual by name. If you don't know who deals with your particular type of work, telephone the office and enquire. Psychologically, this will create a 'plus' in the editor's mind when he picks up your manuscript.

Q. *Are there any unwritten laws about submitting work to a publisher or editor?*

A. Yes. Always enclose either a stamped, self-addressed envelope or stamps to cover the cost of postage should it be returned.

Q. *I have access to a fax machine. Can I fax articles and stories to a magazine?*

A. If your work has been commissioned by an editor, it is possible this method of submission would be acceptable and even preferable, especially if there is a deadline looming. Otherwise, mail it in the normal way.

Q. *How long should I wait before contacting an editor about a story I submitted nearly six weeks previously?*

A.   It is wise to wait for three months. If by that time you have heard nothing, you could write a short, polite letter of enquiry. Never telephone or turn up at the magazine's offices. If you pester them to know the fate of your work, the chances are it will come winging back. However annoyed you may feel at the delay, remember that editors are busy people and, these days, their offices are often seriously understaffed.

Q.   *I've written something with a topical slant. If an editor were to hold on to it for long, it would be too late to submit it elsewhere. How can I get round this?*

A.   State in a covering letter that, because of its topical nature, you require a reply by a specific date, after which time you will feel free to submit it elsewhere.

Q.   *I sent two short stories to a magazine nearly a year ago. I've since written to the editor twice, asking for their return if they didn't wish to use them. Still no reply. What should I do now?*

A.   You should write once more, this time by Recorded Delivery so you have proof of posting. State that, if you have not heard by (state a date, say, two weeks hence), you will assume they are not interested in using your material and will feel free to submit it to another magazine. If this does not bring either a prompt reply or the return of your manuscripts, you can try somewhere else. But make sure you keep your Recorded Delivery slip safe, together with copies of your letters.

Q.   *If I want to submit a story or article to a monthly magazine, how much in advance should it be?*

A.   Material for monthly publications should be sent at least three months ahead of the relevant issue and even earlier if at all possible. Christmas issues tend to be special ones, so for those it is wise to submit material at least six months in advance. The sooner you can get work out, especially if it has a seasonal tie-in, the better your chance of acceptance. And if it is rejected, it gives you more time to try it elsewhere, so improving the odds of success.

Q. *Whom should I address my short story to when I'm submitting to a magazine?*

A. To the fiction editor – but, if possible, find out his/her name and address it personally. Even though you may not send a covering letter (which isn't strictly necessary) and it isn't likely to be the editor who actually opens the mail, none the less it will help create the impression that you have done your homework and studied the magazine.

Q. *Whom should I address my article to at a newspaper or magazine?*

A. To the features editor, who will deal with short non-fiction pieces. If possible, address it personally, otherwise mark it 'For the attention of the Features Editor'.

Q. *I'm about to send my first novel to a publisher. Shall I mention that I intend writing a sequel and possibly a series based on the same main character?*

A. Yes, though it would be best to say you've already started working on the next one, assuming that you have. Publishers and agents alike want to have any relevant information about a potential author's subsequent books and/or ambitions.

Q. *I want to send a story to a US market. Should I change spellings and/or words and expression to the American form – trashcan, sidewalk, elevator, center and so on – where it differs?*

A.   It would be sensible to do so, although if they really liked your story it would not be rejected because of such differences.

Q.   *My novel is set against a background with which I'm familiar (farming). Should I tell the publisher when I send it to him?*

A.   Yes. He will then know the background is authentic.

Q.   *I want to submit an article to a foreign magazine. How do I enclose postage for its possible return?*

A.   Buy International Reply-Paid coupons from the Post Office sufficient to cover cost of return. Alternatively, if you have your work on disk, you can state it isn't necessary to return it, if not accepted, and just enclose one IR coupon for a letter.

Q.   *I've written a story which I consider suitable for a particular magazine but, inside its cover, it states it does not accept unsolicited material. Is there any point in sending it?*

A.   No, but all is not lost. Write a brief letter to the fiction editor (find his/her name and address it personally), something on the lines of:

> Dear Diana Bloggs,
>   I have been studying X magazine and its fiction for several months and have written a 1500-word short story which I believe fits in with your requirements. Although I realise it is not your practice to accept unsolicited material, I wonder if I might send it to you for consideration? I enclose an SAE and look forward to a favourable reply.

By demonstrating, in this way, that you have taken a professional approach and studied the magazine in question, you may well be rewarded with an invitation to submit your story.

Q. *What is a suitable form of address to use when writing to an editor?*

A. Dear George Bloggs/Dear Mary James is the form favoured today, as Mr, Miss or Ms are considered rather formal. Addressing an editor solely by his/her first name might, reasonably, come across as being rather too familiar.

Q. *I've been told this isn't a good time to try to get a novel published. How do I know when I should submit mine?*

A. You don't. The truth is there never *is* a good time. All anyone can do is write to the best of their ability, make sure they send it to the appropriate publisher(s) or agent and, while they are waiting to hear, start work on another. Even though the current climate may not be the best ever for first novelists struggling to break into print, you have to be an optimist or you might as well give up.

Q. *Can I submit the same short story to more than one magazine simultaneously?*

A. Definitely not. If you were to do so and two editors accepted it, you would be placed in the embarrassing position of having to inform one of them that you were withdrawing it. It is unlikely that that editor would ever consider your work again.

Q. *Is there an easy way to count the words in my manuscript?*

A. Most PC software has a facility for this but there is a simple method which is reasonably accurate, bearing in mind that, so far as printing is concerned, a line with only one or two words takes up as much space as a complete line.

1. Count the number of words on each of, say, ten

pages, including words of one or two letters.

2. Count the lines on a page (this should be consistent throughout).

3. Add the total number of words on those ten pages, then divide by ten. This will give you the number of words per page.

4. Multiply the number of pages in the MS by the number of words per page which will give you the length.

COPING WITH REJECTION

Q. *I've had my novel returned by nine publishers and I feel like giving up. At what point should I accept that I don't have enough talent to become a writer?*

A. Whilst talent is necessary to become a writer, of equal importance is a determination to succeed. If you are prepared to persevere and to learn your craft, you will considerably increase your chances of seeing your work in print one day.

Margaret Thomson Davies had eight novels rejected in turn, including a trilogy which a publisher returned after keeping them for nine months. Her innate determination having come to the fore, however, she had completed two more by then. She submitted these last two to the publisher who had rejected the trilogy. Within a week, they had replied saying they had decided to publish all five! Proof, surely, that perseverance pays in the end.

Q. *Do publishers read every manuscript they receive?*

A. Yes, though not necessarily all of it because it will usually be clear from the first pages if it is worthy of serious consideration. This reinforces the advice so often given as to the importance of the first chapter and, even more so, the first three pages. Time spent on making the opening of a novel as compelling as possible will ensure that a publisher reads on.

Q. *Why don't publishers or editors say why they are rejecting a story?*

A. It is simply a matter of time and economics. Nowadays, with office staff reduced to a minimum, few editors have the time or personnel available to do more than return unsuitable material with a standard rejection letter or slip.

Q. *My novel came back from a publisher with some extremely nice comments: interesting story, enjoyed reading it, attractively written and so on, but ... I then sent it to another with much the same result. Why?*

A. There seems to be a belief among many publishers that they must be kind to aspiring novelists. Thus, instead of being honest (which is possible without being cruel) and merely stating that the book was not suitable for them or that, in their opinion, it was not up to publishable standard, too often they try to let the author down lightly, which can fill him with unrealistic hope.

Q. *After how many rejections should I consider an article or story unsaleable and bin it?*

A. First, *never* throw away any piece of writing as you never know when you might be able to re-use it or cannibalise it. Second, if it has been rejected several times, ask yourself (a) Have you been sending it to the right markets? (b) Are you sure it is sufficiently well written? To answer both questions honestly, do some more market study and, if possible, put the piece away for a few weeks, then take it out again and look at it objectively. If you are sure it cannot be improved, send it out again, because it will never sell sitting on your desk. While you are waiting to hear if it has been accepted or rejected, get on with another. If you always have one or more article or story out, it will soften the blow of rejection if one comes back.

Q. *I've had some half-dozen stories rejected by the same editor, over the past year. Is there any point in continuing to aim at that magazine or do you think I've been blacklisted?*

A. This is almost certainly not the case. Probably, it is simply that the material you have submitted is unsuitable; nothing to do with the sight of your name on the manuscript. However, it might be wise to take a fresh, hard look at that particular market and try to see where you are going wrong. Analyse both the magazine itself and the stories in it over several issues, then try again.

Q. *A magazine rejected a story of mine more than a year ago. Since then, the editor has changed and I'm wondering if it would be worth my submitting it again?*

A. You have nothing to lose in doing so. Editors have their personal preferences, like anyone else, and it may be that another will like it and accept it. You might consider changing the title before sending it out a second time, though.

Q. *I've had a story returned with a letter of rejection but adding that the editor would be pleased to see any other material. Is that just a standard, polite letter or does it mean what it says?*

A. It means what it says. No editor takes the time and trouble to ask would-be contributors to send in more work unless he believes there is a chance they might be successful next time. Don't rush it, though. Take sufficient time to ensure the next story is as good as you can possibly make it and is right for the magazine.

Q. *Recently, I sent out a story and received a slip which stated it was being considered. Is that a hopeful sign?*

A. Not necessarily. It may be standard practice to acknowledge receipt of manuscripts and so this should not be interpreted as indicating likely acceptance.

Q. *A writer acquaintance of mine told me that he had sold an article after it had been rejected nineteen times. How could the same piece have been suitable for twenty different markets?*

A. It's possible that some of the markets he aimed at were not right for his material, which is why it was rejected so many times. It is also possible he re-wrote it, giving it another slant, before submitting it again, though a piece aimed at one market might also be suitable for several others in terms of length and subject matter. What comes over, more than anything else, is his determination and persistence in sending it out rather than giving up and filing it away under the heading 'Rejected Material'.

Q. *Have you any suggestions for dealing with the despair one feels after having had a story or novel rejected?*

A. Once you have recovered from the initial disappointment, as soon as possible go to your nearest bookshop/library/newsagent (depending upon the work rejected) and buy/borrow a book of the same genre as your own or the latest issue of the magazine at which you were aiming. On returning home, sit down and analyse it in depth and as objectively as possible. Try to see how your story differed in terms of plot structure, number of characters and the way they were portrayed, amount of dialogue and action and so on.

If you tackle rejection in a positive light, seeing it as an inevitable step on the way to success, you will learn from it. Once you can see some of the flaws in your own story, you should not make the same mistakes again and so will be further along the road to becoming a successful writer.

SUMMING UP

You have now realised you are not alone in having to cope with rejection. You have learned how to give yourself the best chance of having your work accepted as a result of painstaking revision and market study. But you want to know what other considerations are involved. And so we move on to the final stage, which will tie up the loose ends and answer all those other questions that plague you.

Getting into Print

You have had your first acceptance and, consequently, your confidence in yourself as a writer has received an enormous boost. But you wonder how you stand in respect of copyright, of obtaining permission for quoting others, of working with an editor, publisher or maybe a literary agent. What about legal or tax problems? Should you ever pay to see your work in print?

In this last section, we will take a practical and pragmatic look at issues such as these because they, too, need to be considered and understood.

WRITERS' JARGON

Q. *What is a deadline?*

A. It is the time/date set by an editor or publisher when they expect to receive the piece of writing for which they have contracted.

Q. *What is a book-packager?*

A. A book-packager is a comparatively new phenomenon in the publishing world. He is a middleman who buys a book (usually either non-fiction or, sometimes, children's books) from the author. He normally, though not always, pays an outright fee, and an author might be able to negotiate a share of royalties. The packager arranges for the printing, then sells the complete package to a publisher. He will also provide the illustrations, where appropriate.

Q. *What is a 'kill fee'?*

A. This is the fee paid for a short piece of writing which has been accepted but which, for whatever reason, will not appear in print. This might be because the publication has since folded, changed editor or changed its policy. The fee may, or may not, be the same as the one originally agreed but it should leave the author free to offer the piece elsewhere, though if he has received the full fee, he should check on this. It is always possible the publication will want to retain the rights for a specified period in case they decide to use it later.

Q. *What is meant by 'author intrusion'?*

A. It is when, in a work of fiction, there is a comment in the narrative which is clearly not being made by the character involved but is from 'outside'. In effect, the author has intruded. A crude example would be: 'Little did he know then that, before the year was out, Mary would be completely in charge of the factory.'

Q. *What is meant by unsolicited material?*

A. Work which has not been commissioned by an editor or publisher.

Q. *What is a ghost writer?*

A. This is someone who writes up another person's story in saleable form. Sometimes their name appears on the book jacket in the form of 'as told to . . .' or 'with . . .' but often it does not.

Q. *What is interior monologue?*

A. This is the putting down of a character's thoughts in a stream-of-consciousness form of narrative rather than in dialogue form. It was sometimes used by James Joyce and by Virginia Woolf.

Q. *What is PLR (Public Lending Right)?*

A. This is the scheme (which came into operation in 1984) whereby every author whose full-length book is registered for the scheme receives a yearly sum from government funding. It is based on the estimated number of times the book is borrowed from a public library, being calculated by taking a random sample of twenty different libraries each year. It came into being as a result of persistent action by the Society of Authors and the Writers' Guild of Great Britain.

Q. *How do I know if I'm eligible for PLR and, if I am, how do I register for it?*

A. To qualify for PLR, a book must have an ISBN (International Standard Book Number), as only those with one are available in public libraries. You can apply for one to the ISBN Agency, 12 Dyott Street, London WC1A 1DF, although publishing houses do this automatically. You then register for PLR through the Public Lending Right Office (see Useful Addresses, p. 196).

Q. *What is the Net Book Agreement?*

A. The Net Book Agreement was drawn up between publishers and booksellers to ensure that books could not be sold for less than the cover price, except under special conditions such as those negotiated between the publisher and a book club. However, in 1994 and 1995 a number of major publishing houses withdrew from the Net Book Agreement and 'de-netted' their titles, leaving booksellers free to set their own prices. This means that the Agreement has in effect collapsed, although some publishers continue to support the principle behind it. At the time of writing, book jackets continue to bear the publishers' *recommended* retail price (RRP); whether they will do so in the future is a matter of intense debate. Watch this space!

Q. *What is a print run?*

A. This is the number of copies of a book produced at any one time by the publisher.

Q. *What is 'remaindering'?*

A. If a publisher decides that he cannot sell any more copies of a particular book, he will sell them off at a fraction of the published price. This practice is known as remaindering. Remaindered books are usually sold in 'cut-price' book shops but, first, they will have been offered to the author as stipulated in most contracts.

Q. *What is 'faction'?*

A. It is the relatively new term coined to describe a work which is a blend of fact and fiction.

Q. *What is the Minimum Terms Agreement?*

A. This ensures that an author's contract offers what are considered to be the minimum acceptable terms. Drawn up by the Society of Authors in collaboration with the Writers' Guild, it is now adhered to by most bona fide publishers.

Q. *What is a trade paperback?*

A. The paperback edition of a non-fiction book.

Q. *What is plagiarism?*

A. Passing off another writer's work as your own. In effect, it involves stealing someone else's copyright. Although there is no copyright in ideas, if you deliberately used another writer's plot (this would not apply if it was out of copyright, that is, fifty years after the author's death) for your own novel, and it was clearly recognisable, you would run the risk of being sued for breach of copyright.

Q. *What is meant by 'on spec'?*

A. When a writer offers an idea for an article to an editor and is not given a definite commission, merely the opportunity to submit it in the hope that it will prove suitable, he will be submitting it 'on spec' (which is short for 'on speculation'). In other words, no contract was made to publish the finished piece. However, if a new writer is invited to submit work 'on spec', he should welcome it because, if successful, it could lead to other opportunities.

Q. *What do 'payment on acceptance' and 'payment on publication' mean?*

A. These terms refer to the time element before a writer receives payment for a particular piece. Some publications pay soon after written acceptance of a piece has been made (probably at the end of that month) while others do not pay until the end of the month in which it appears in print. Obviously, it is to the writer's advantage to be paid as soon as his work has been accepted, but he will not be able to change the magazine's policy and can only abide by its stated terms.

Q. *What is a 'slush pile'?*

A. It is the somewhat derogatory term for those novels

155

which are sent direct to a publisher by a writer without being requested. When a novel is submitted by an agent, the publisher assumes it will be of publishable standard and so will take a closer look at it. If it merely arrives in the day's post, it will be put into the 'slush pile' to await a more cursory glance. Thus, whenever possible, it pays to try to find a way to avoid your work ending up there.

Q.   *What is meant by the term 'multiple submission'?*

A.   It is when the same manuscript is sent to more than one publisher at the same time. In the UK, articles and short stories should *never* be sent, simultaneously, to more than one publication though it is now widely accepted that novels may be, provided each publisher is informed of this.

Q.   *What is a sidebar?*

A.   This is the short, associated item, often in bold type, placed alongside a news report or feature, thus breaking up one long piece into smaller segments.

Q.   *What is a 'cliff-hanger'?*

A.   It is the term used to describe a peak of suspense or tension at the end of a chapter or instalment of a magazine/TV/radio serial which, metaphorically, leaves the reader/viewer/listener 'in the air' until the next instalment.

Q.   *What is meant by the expression 'hype'?*

A.   Short for 'hyperbole', it has come to mean, in the publishing world, extensive advertising of a new book.

Q.   *What is meant by 'anthropomorphic'?*

A. It means giving animal characters human emotions.

Q. *I've heard about 'stream-of-consciousness' writing but I don't understand what it means. Can you explain?*

A. It is writing which has no definite structure but merely flows from the author's pen (or machine) without conscious direction, often stemming from a word or phrase. It is a useful method for getting rid of writer's block, letting the unconscious produce the writing without striving after it.

Q. *What is a sub-plot and how does it differ from the main plot?*

A. A sub-plot should stem from the main plot of a novel and have some bearing on what happens to the main characters. For instance, in a murder mystery, there might be a sub-plot in which a suspect is involved in a love affair which could affect his/her behaviour. Normally, it will not have any direct influence on the main story but will enrich it.

Q. *What do the initials aka mean?*

A. They stand for 'also known as'.

Q. *What is a tear-sheet?*

A. It literally means the page torn from a magazine in which your story or article appears which you send to an editor as an example of your work.

Q. *What is a blurb?*

A. It is the brief résumé of a book which appears on its cover. It is written with the specific purpose of persuading potential purchasers to buy the book.

Q. *What is an imprint?*

A. It is the name given to a specific publishing venture. There are often several separate imprints under the umbrella of one publishing house. For example, they may publish one or more series of children's books which will come out as a particular imprint. Virgin Publishing not so long ago launched their Black Lace imprint for erotic writing aimed at women. Random House have their Arrow paperback imprint, among others. Any author wishing to self-publish can choose an imprint for their own work and can check that no one else is using it by contacting Companies House, Crown Way, Cardiff CF4 3UZ, Tel: Cardiff 01222 388588.

WORKING WITH EDITOR AND PUBLISHER

Promoting Books

Q. *I'm rather shy and am concerned that I will be expected to appear in public to help promote my book. Am I worrying about this unnecessarily?*

A. Indeed, yes. Obviously, if you have the sort of outgoing personality which thrives on publicity, it makes sense to be seen as often as possible in connection with your book. In reality, unless it turns out to be a bestseller, such opportunities are likely to be few and far between, but in any case no one will try to make you undertake engagements of this nature.

Jackets

Q. *Can I make suggestions for the jacket of my book?*

A. There is no reason why you should not make your editor aware of your ideas but it is unlikely much attention will be paid to them. Normally, publishers employ specialist artists to design book jackets.

Q. *What if I don't like the illustrations for the dustjacket of my book? Can I tell the editor and will he take any notice?*

A. Out of courtesy, you should be sent a proof of your book's jacket before it goes to the printer. If you have strong and reasonable objections, such as that your heroine's hair is blonde but the cover shows her as a brunette, you would have grounds for complaint. But merely not liking the cover would not be sufficient reason to expect it to be changed.

Q. *Will I be expected to write the blurb for the cover of my book?*

A. Some publishers ask the author to provide the blurb but most do not. As it is a sales ploy to encourage potential readers to purchase the book, it is probably best written by people with sales and marketing experience.

Q. *My first children's book is coming out shortly, and I'm wondering if I ought to try to promote it myself, locally – or should I leave all that to my publishers?*

A. Most publishers have a specific department which will arrange as much publicity as is practicable, given their likely budget restrictions. However, they will be more than willing for you to do some promoting yourself once the book is actually out. For instance, you might be prepared to mailshot friends and colleagues and perhaps also schools and libraries in the area. It would also be worth asking your publisher if they have contacted local newspapers and radio station(s) and, if they haven't, offer to do so. 'Local author's success' stories are usually welcomed by the media in the area where he/she lives.

Editorial Changes

Q. *What if I disagree with the editor over something in my book?*

A. It is important to have a good working relationship with your editor and you should feel able to discuss any points of disagreement. A good editor will always listen to an author's point of view. If you feel strongly about the issue, stand your ground. However, remember an editor can look at the book far more objectively than the author and so you would be wise to consider his ideas carefully before dismissing them.

Q. *I was extremely annoyed to find that my story had been severely edited before it appeared in print. Should I complain to the editor?*

A. That depends upon how strongly you feel about the editing, how keen you are to have your work appear in that magazine in the future and whether you signed a contract which stipulated there might be editorial changes. You could write a polite letter to the editor concerned, saying you weren't too happy with the sub-editing and asking what the reasons were, in order to help you get it right in future. That way, you will let them know that you noticed, did not approve but are willing to learn more about their particular requirements.

Q. *Has an editor the right to make changes in my material without consulting me first?*

A. In so far as a magazine editor is concerned, generally speaking, yes. The reason is that they are often working to a tight deadline and might not have time to write to you first. It is one of those things which the freelance fiction writer has to accept. In non-fiction, however, this is not so likely to happen as the author, presumably, will be writing as an expert on a specific subject.

Q. *Do editors often change titles? As I spend a long time searching for what I consider to be a good one, it's extremely irritating when it's changed.*

A. Titles are often changed by editors for various reasons. It may be they used a similar one to yours recently, or have another in the pipeline. But it may simply be that the editor did not like it or felt a different one would be more appropriate.

Q. *I've heard about editors wanting changes to a book after contracts have been signed and the manuscript completed. How many can I expect to have to make and have I the right to refuse?*

A. No editor will want to make changes for the sake of it. He will only ask for them for a specific and definite reason – he may ask you to rewrite something which might possibly be libellous, for example. As to the type of amendment requested, this will vary and depend upon the book in question. Your contract will almost certainly contain a clause to the effect that you must make any alterations and amendments requested by the publisher.

In most cases, it is wise to accept an editor's advice as this is likely to improve a book. However, if you disagree strongly, discuss it with your editor, who will be prepared to listen to your arguments. But if agreement cannot be reached, remember the editor's decision is final and the end result might be the cancellation of your contract and the non-publication of your book.

Q. *What is a sub-editor?*

A. A newspaper or magazine sub-editor is not a deputy editor. His/her job is to edit the material before it goes to the printer, correcting grammatical and spelling errors, perhaps moving pieces of text around or cutting where necessary. The equivalent person in book-publishing is called a copy-editor.

PUBLISHER'S READER

Q. *What is a publisher's reader and what is his function?*

A. This is someone employed specifically to read manuscripts sent in to the publisher. He will make a brief report on each book, recommending either that it should be rejected or that it should go on to the next stage, when it will be read by an editor before a final decision is taken.

Publishers' readers are mainly concerned with first novels rather than non-fiction books because, in order to be considered, the novel needs to have been completed, whereas a non-fiction book may only be in outline form at the point of approaching a publisher.

Q. *I'd like to become a publisher's reader. How do I go about it and what qualifications would I need?*

A. You would have to have considerable experience as either a writer or an editor. In other words, you need to be knowledgeable about fiction-writing. If you believe you have the right background, write to the publisher of your choice, detailing your experience in the field of fiction, and offer your services.

Q. *At what point in my writing career can I expect to be commissioned for work by an editor?*

A. That will depend on individual editors and the amount of work you have already done for them. If you specialise in a particular area, you may be commissioned for specific features. But there is no hard and fast rule.

LITERARY AGENTS

Q. *I've completed my first novel and would like an agent to handle it for me. How do I go about finding one?*

A. *The Writer's Handbook* and *The Writers' and Artists' Year Book* list most of the bona fide agents in the UK and you can write to any of them (unless they specify they are not taking on new clients). Most prefer a preliminary letter, giving brief details of your book, its length, category and so on. They will also want to know of any successes you may have had (for instance, if you have sold a number of magazine stories or won a national writing competition), something of your writing ambitions and if you are working on your next book. Other agents state they want these details plus the first three chapters and synopsis of your book.

However, it is notoriously as difficult to find an agent willing to take on a new writer as it is to find a publisher and by far the best way is through a personal introduction, perhaps by an established writer. Attending writers' conferences and seminars at which an agent is speaking is also helpful because it may then be possible to make a personal approach, yourself. Here again, persistence often pays off and you shouldn't give up at the first refusal as there are a large number of agents operating in the UK.

Q. *I approached a literary agent and asked if he would consider taking me on and trying to sell my first novel. I've now been asked for a reading fee. Is this normal or ethical?*

A. Because of the increasing number of aspiring novelists approaching them, a few reputable agents now ask for a small reading fee or contribution towards editorial costs. If looked at objectively, this is a not unreasonable demand because of the amount of work involved. *The Writer's Handbook* and *The Writers' and Artists' Year Book* usually state which agents do not request a reading fee and it is up to you to decide if you want to pay such a fee.

Q.   *What exactly does a literary agent do for an author?*

A.   First of all, an agent will try to find a publisher for your work. If he is successful, he will then negotiate the best possible contract for you in terms of advance and royalties. Where possible, he will attempt to sell foreign rights, film and television rights, if appropriate, and any other subsidiary rights. Secondly, a good agent should offer some editorial advice which may help an author improve his book. Thirdly, he will be responsible for collecting all monies due to the author and accounting to him for these.

Q.   *What fee does a literary agent charge?*

A.   He will take a commission from all monies received on the basis of an already agreed figure. This varies from agent to agent but the norm for UK sales is between ten and fifteen per cent, with the higher figure becoming more and more usual nowadays, as they have to work harder than ever to place work, in the current economic climate. In respect of overseas sales, the commission may be somewhat higher.

Q.   *A literary agent has agreed to act for me in selling my work. Will I have to sign a contract binding me to him, in the same way as I would sign a contract with a publisher?*

A.   It is not normal for there to be a formal, written contract between an agent and an author. However, it is wise for it to be clear from the outset exactly what the agent will be undertaking for you and what you will be paying him. For instance, it is possible you may wish to sell some of your work yourself (short stories, for instance, or a work of non-fiction as opposed to your normal fiction) and you will need to come to an agreement in such a case.

Q. *I've just obtained a contract for my first novel and I'm wondering if I should now try to find an agent, both for this book and for any subsequent ones?*

A. As you have negotiated your own contract for your first book, provided you are happy with the terms you have obtained it may be that you do not need an agent. However, if you feel you would prefer to have one act for you in the future, now would be a good time to approach one. You should not have too much difficulty in finding one willing to represent you as you have proved yourself a successful author. In the meantime, it would be sensible to join an organisation such as the Society of Authors or, if you are a woman, the Society of Women Writers and Journalists.

Q. *I've had a literary agent for the past three years but am increasingly disenchanted and now wish to move to another. Will my original agent still be entitled to commission on any of my work?*

A. Legally, your old agent will be entitled to commission on any work for which he negotiated a contract on your behalf. Your new one, however, will expect to receive commission on any contracts he negotiates.

Q. *Is there an association which sets out a code of practice for literary agents?*

A. Yes. The Association of Authors' Agents (the AAA) is a professional association to which most literary agents in the UK belong.

Q. *Is having work handled by a literary agent purely a business arrangement?*

A.   No, it is normally more than that. Most agents say that there must be a rapport between them and their authors or it would be impossible to represent them. Authors have to be able to trust their agent to be doing as much as possible for them. If that trust is no longer there, it would be better to move to another firm.

Q.   *Are there any agents who only handle short stories?*

A.   No, because there would be too little financial reward from short stories only. However, if an agent takes on a novelist who also writes short stories, he will almost certainly try to place those with suitable magazines.

Q.   *Is it all right to approach more than one agent at once, asking if they will handle my book?*

A.   This is not considered ethical. You should write to one at a time.

Q.   *How long should I expect to wait before I hear whether an agent is willing to put me on his list?*

A.   Two months is a reasonable time by which to receive a reply. If you haven't heard by then, chase it up and/or ask for your manuscript to be returned.

CONTRACTS

Q.   *I find I'm getting behind on my work schedule for a book and it looks as though I shan't be able to finish it by the time stipulated in the contract. What should I do?*

A.   Get in touch with your publishers immediately and let them know the situation. Most of them will be understanding about this sort of problem and are likely to be cooperative. In any case, if you read your contract carefully, it will probably contain a clause to the effect that you have been allowed a period of grace (usually three months) to cover possible delay in producing a manuscript by the specified date.

Q. *I've had a short story accepted and received a contract which states the magazine is buying All Rights. As I stipulated First British Serial Rights only when I submitted my story, what should I do?*

A. The magazine in question is probably hoping you will sign away all rights to your story without objection. However, if you do not want to do this and made it clear in writing that you were offering only First Rights, the simplest way of dealing with it is to cross out the words All Rights, substitute First British Serial Rights, initial the alteration and return the contract. As a precaution, keep a photocopy for your files in case of any dispute in the future. In fact, that is likely to be the end of the matter.

Q. *I've just received a contract for my first book but I haven't got an agent and feel I need someone experienced to check it for me. Is there anyone I can approach?*

A. Having received a contract for a full-length work, you are eligible to join the Society of Authors who will vet it for you free of charge. The Society was instrumental in persuading a large number of publishers to accept what is known as the Minimum Terms Agreement, which sets out what are considered to be fair and reasonable terms in an author's contract. Even if you are not a member of the Society at present, you may still approach them and ask if they would look at the contract for you. They are sometimes accommodating over this but, in any case, for a small fee you may obtain from them a copy of the Minimum Terms Agreement so that you can compare it with your own contract.

Q. *There are a few changes I'd like to make to my contract for a book. How should I go about this and is my publisher likely to object?*

A. Write to your publisher, setting out the changes you wish to make. If they are fair and reasonable, they are unlikely to object. If they do, they should give an explanation and it is then up to you to take the matter further or accept their conditions.

Q. *Will I be able to buy copies of my book at a discount from my publisher?*

A. Invariably, yes, and it should state this in your contract. The normal author's discount is one-third of the published price.

Q. *Will I be able to sell copies of my book at less than cover price?*

A. Since the Net Book Agreement is no longer supported by many publishers, booksellers are able to discount books and sell them at less than their cover price. However, publishing policy in this area is not set in stone and it may well be that your publisher is not happy for you to make a similar arrangement. You would need to clarify the situation with your particular publisher; you could make it a negotiating point when discussing the terms of your contract.

Q. *What is the normal period between the signing of a contract and the book being published?*

A. It varies, but each contract will stipulate the time by which a publisher agrees to publish a book after receipt of the manuscript and its final acceptance. The period most commonly stated is eighteen months.

Q. *I've just heard that my book has been accepted. Will the publisher expect me to offer him my next book or will I be free to send it to another?*

A. Your contract will undoubtedly contain a clause stipu-
lating that you must offer your next book (and possibly
the next two) to them. This is known as the Option
Clause. Generally speaking, publishers do not want
one-book authors because it often takes time to build
them up until they become known to the book-buying
public who then look for their books. The publisher
expects sales to increase with each subsequent book
and so, quite reasonably, views the author as an invest-
ment.

Q. *How long will I be given to finish my book after signing the
contract?*

A. Normally, you should expect to be allowed at least six
months but that is something to be negotiated between
you and the publisher. If there is a strong topical
element involved, it is possible they will want the manuscript produced within a shorter period of, say, three
months. On the other hand, if the book involves a
considerable amount of research, you may need considerably longer.

Q. *I understand an author receives a number of free copies of his
book on publication. How many can I expect?*

A. Most contracts stipulate that the author shall receive six
free copies of his book upon publication. Normally, he
will get these a few weeks before they actually appear in
the bookshops.

Q. *What rights will a publisher want when I sign the contract for
my first book?*

A. He will want sole and exclusive rights to publish the
book in the English language either throughout the
world or in the UK and Commonwealth. In effect, an
author grants a publisher a licence to publish his book,

169

this licence to extend for a specified number of years, likely to be a minimum of five.

Q. *Will I have to proofread my book before it's published?*

A. It is usual for an author to be expected to check the proofs of his book before it finally goes to print. Normally this is not a difficult task but it is essential to make sure there are no glaring errors in the text or any grammatical or spelling mistakes which have been over-looked in the editing. You will not be allowed to make any other changes to the actual text, however, without incurring the typesetting costs yourself. Most contracts stipulate that the cost of amending errors of over ten per cent of the book after it has been typeset must be borne by the author.

Q. *Would I be penalised if, for any reason, I'm unable to finish my book on time, for example, if I were taken ill?*

A. If you were *unavoidably* prevented from producing the manuscript of your book for substantially longer than stated in your contract (through illness or hospitalisa-tion, for instance), most publishers would be sympathetic and allow you sufficient extra time to complete the book. The important thing is to make sure they are aware of the situation as soon as it arises.

Q. *How does a publisher decide on the advance an author will be paid?*

A. This will depend largely on how successful he thinks the book is likely to be. A rough-and-ready calculation can be made by multiplying the proposed print run (say, 3000 copies) by the royalty percentage of the antici-pated cover price. Two-thirds of the resulting figure will give an approximation of the advance. Thus, 3000 copies at a cover price of £10 and with a royalty of ten per cent should mean an advance of £2000 for the author.

Q. *How is a book advance paid?*

A. Normally, it is paid in three parts. The first part is payable when the contract is signed, the second when the completed manuscript is received *and approved* by the publisher, and the last part should be paid by the end of the month in which the book is published.

Q. *What are normal royalties for a hardback?*

A. A ten per cent royalty is the norm for hardback copies sold through bookshops. Copies sold to a book club or similar outlet will carry lower royalties.

Q. *What royalties can I expect for a paperback edition of my book?*

A. Usually, paperback editions will start at seven and a half per cent.

Q. *How soon after publication can I expect to receive royalties?*

A. There is no definite answer to this as it depends upon how successful your book is. You will not receive any royalty payment until the amount of the advance has been recouped from sales. Thus, the bigger the advance obtained, the longer it is likely you will have to wait before receiving further payment.

Q. *How often are royalties paid?*

A. Most contracts state that royalties will be paid twice yearly.

Q. *If my book does not earn the advance I was paid, will I have to pay any of it back?*

A. No. Your publisher took a calculated risk, when making you an advance, that it would be covered by the book's sales. If it isn't, that is his loss, not yours.

Q. *I think my book would benefit from having an index. Will I be expected to bear the cost of this?*

A. Almost certainly your contract will stipulate that an index will be the author's responsibility. You will have to pay a professional indexer to prepare it for you or else undertake the task yourself, which can be quite time-consuming.

Q. *My book has been accepted and the publisher wants it to have an index. According to my contract, it is up to me to do it myself or pay for it. Is there any way round this, as I don't want to undertake this work or to have to pay a professional to do it?*

A. When you signed your contract, you agreed to this. However, you might consider suggesting that the book does not need an index.

SELF/VANITY/SUBSIDY PUBLISHING

Q. *I've been warned not to consider vanity publishing, but what is the difference between that and self-publishing?*

A. There are two main differences. The first is that with self-publishing the author retains full control of the operation. The second is that it will cost considerably less than if he uses a vanity publisher.

Q. *What does self-publishing entail and how much work is involved?*

A. There are three methods of self-publishing. The simplest and cheapest is to use the services of a small printer who will quote you for typesetting, printing and, if you wish, binding a set number of copies of your book. In other words, it will be a straightforward business arrangement and you will get exactly what you agree to pay for. He will not undertake any marketing or advertising or obtain reviews of your book and, once he hands over the printed and bound copies, his part in the procedure is at an end.

The second method entails a great deal more work on your part and should be considered only if you are prepared for this and, preferably, can draw on help from someone with experience in publishing. It involves your hiring the typesetter, choosing and purchasing the paper, deciding on the cover, on any illustrations used and paying for it to be bound. You will then have to market it yourself and send out any review copies.

The third method will involve you in less work than the second but will cost more because it means using the services of a middleman. At present there is at least one reputable entrepreneurial company specialising in self-publishing which offers this middle way. But, as always, before parting with large sums of money, you should check on the financial status of any firm or association with which you are dealing. Some time ago, an association in business to self-publish individual authors' work went into liquidation, leaving many authors with no books and having lost large amounts of money.

Q. *I've tried without success to find a publisher for my novel and I'm now considering trying one of the so-called vanity or subsidy publishers. If I do, might it help me to interest a bona fide publisher afterwards?*

A. No. In fact, the opposite is likely to be the case as it would advertise to a bona fide publisher that your book had not been considered good enough for anyone else to take. They would be well aware that you had had to pay for it to appear in print.

Q. *How do I decide whether or not to self-publish my book?*

A. First of all, ask yourself how important it is to see your work in print and how much money you are willing to risk in case you don't recoup all your expenses. Next, think about possible markets for your book. Who is likely to want to read it? Will it have a small specialist readership or a much wider appeal? You need to work out, realistically, how many copies you are likely to sell in order to decide on how many to have printed. This figure will affect the total cost and also the price at which you can sell it (the bigger the print run, the lower the cost per copy). You must also consider how much time and effort you are prepared to put into promoting and marketing it, because it won't sell itself.

But self-publishing is a highly suitable method for certain types of books which a commercial publisher would not be able to consider because of their limited market: for instance, a small one about local walks or maybe a cookery book based on recipes from a specific region. (You would almost certainly have to publish these without colour photographs, as these would increase the cost considerably.)

Whilst self-publishing is undoubtedly a growth area and an option many authors are now considering, the key to the whole question of whether to go this route is knowing to whom you can expect to sell the book. And, although there have been a few notable success stories where a self-published book has subsequently been taken up by a commercial publisher and brought fame and considerable financial reward to its author, these are the exception and it would not be sensible to anticipate the same result for your own. In the end, it comes back to the first part of this answer: how much do you want to see your work in print?

Q. *I answered an advertisement in the national press which invited new authors to submit work, and sent off my novel, full of hope. I got an enthusiastic letter (my manuscript wasn't returned) saying that, contrary to popular belief, a good book will not necessarily always find a publisher, but they considered mine was worthy of publication. They suggested a commercial enterprise in which I, as the author, would put up part of the considerable sum required to publish it. I am reluctant to enter into such an arrangement unless I can be fairly certain of recouping this money. Am I likely to do so and are such publishers genuine?*

A. The answer to the first part of your question is a definite 'No'. The chances of a book published in this way (known as vanity or subsidy publishing) selling enough copies to pay for itself are extremely slim. The answer to the second part is that such publishers are genuine in that they are usually legitimate companies but they are prone to making unrealistic promises, offering false praise of work submitted in order to obtain a contract.

Before making any commitment, you should ask to see a sample specimen of a similar book they have published which would show the quality, style and appearance you could expect for yours. If you are satisfied with this, and certainly before parting with any money, you should read the proposed contract carefully and make sure you know exactly what you will be receiving in return for your money before you sign it. For instance, make sure you know how many *bound* copies you will receive and if your manuscript will be properly edited to ensure that, at least, any spelling and grammatical errors are corrected (editing is a vital part of the publishing process). Unless you take these precautions, you may find yourself disappointed with both your book and the services received.

COPYRIGHT

Ideas

Q. *Some time ago, I completed a novel based on a true-to-life background of which I had considerable knowledge. After it had been rejected by two publishers, I tried a specialist magazine which, despite repeated requests, never sent it back. Recently, I read a paperback novel by an author who contributes regularly to that magazine, and was horrified to find it was clearly based on my own novel. What can I do to obtain redress?*

A. Proving your story was stolen by someone else is likely to be both difficult and expensive. Was it yours, practically word for word, or was it merely based on your plot? If the former, and you have a copy of your typescript and can prove it pre-dated the publication of the novel (was it lodged with a bank or was a copy sent to yourself by registered post, for example?), you should have a strong legal case. If that is the situation, consult either a lawyer specialising in copyright or publishing matters, or seek advice from the Society of Authors. Even if you are not a member of the Society, they are usually willing to offer advice.

If you believe the novel was based largely on your own plot, you would have a more difficult task to prove it had been stolen. Some time ago, a well-known novelist started legal proceedings against another writer, alleging theft of a plot. The case was dropped before it ever came to court when the defendant was able to show she had, in fact, based her story on a plot long out of copyright.

Bear in mind that there is no copyright in *ideas* and it is not impossible for two writers to have a similar one at the same time. In your particular case, there must be grounds for suspicion that the novelist in question had had sight of your typescript, realised its potential as a good story and decided to use it. But this does not mean it would be easy to prove and could involve you in a costly lawsuit.

Q. *I submitted an idea for a feature to a magazine editor but it was rejected. A few months later, however, they printed an article covering the same topic, and I feel certain my idea was stolen. Is there anything I can do about it?*

A. The chances are that this particular magazine was already considering a similar idea, either previously suggested by another freelance or to be written up by a staff writer, when yours arrived on the editor's desk. Because there is no copyright in ideas, it would be impossible to bring a successful lawsuit for theft unless a large part of the piece you had submitted was used, almost word for word.

Q. *At my writers' group, I mentioned I was writing a feature on a particular subject. A short while later, another member announced he had sold an article on the same subject to the same market I was aiming at. Have I any redress?*

A. As already stated, there is no copyright in ideas. When a group of writers gather together to 'talk shop', it is very easy for an idea to drop into someone's subconscious and, later, when the time is ripe, for it to re-emerge as one they believe they have just thought up. You can only treat this incident as part of the learning process. In future, do not discuss your work with anyone until it is completed and ready for submission. It would then be too late for someone either to steal the idea or to use it, even subconsciously.

Titles

Q. *Is there any copyright in titles? I've just finished a novel and given it what I consider to be a perfect title but, to my chagrin,*

I find there is another book with the same title. Does that matter or can I keep the one I've chosen?

A. There is no copyright in titles but, if the existing book appeared fairly recently and was of the same genre as yours, you might run the risk of legal action for trying to pass your novel off as a bestseller, for instance, or if the title was associated in the public's mind with a well-known author. However, if the published book and your own are of two quite different genres, or if the first is no longer in print, you may be able to keep your title, though if your book is accepted your publisher may prefer you to change it. At this stage, go with the one you want – time enough to consider the situation, should it arise, later.

Competitions

Q. *A poem I entered in a national competition won a prize and subsequently appeared in a small, privately published anthology. Is the copyright still mine and can I submit it elsewhere in the hope of wider publication?*

A. Unless the competition rules demanded the copyright of poems entered, it remains yours. If that is the case, you can offer it for publication elsewhere, but you should state where it has previously appeared.

Protection

Q. *I've written a pilot episode for a TV sitcom and want to protect my copyright before submitting it to a television company. How should I do this?*

A. The two simplest methods are:

- Post a copy to yourself by registered post.
- Lodge a copy with your bank.

Both methods will have proof of date and, in the event of a lawsuit relating to the theft of your work, would stand you in good stead.

Q. *I'd always believed that copyright laws protected someone's work for fifty years after publication but I've been told, recently, that that isn't so. What is the legal position?*

A. Until recently, UK Copyright Law stated that copyright in a piece of writing remained with the author or his heirs for fifty years after his/her death and *not*, as is often erroneously believed, after publication of the work. From 1 July 1995, however, following the European Directive on the Duration of Copyright, the period of time is *seventy* years and not fifty.

Q. *If I don't put the symbol © to denote the copyright of a particular piece of writing belongs to me, does that affect it legally?*

A. The symbol © merely makes a statement that the copyright belongs to you. It is the formal copyright notice agreed by more than sixty countries who are members of the Universal Copyright Convention. But the fact that you wrote it means that in law you are the owner of the copyright and no one can use all or part of it without your permission.

Quotations

Q. *I want to include a line from a famous song in one of my short stories. Can I do so without infringing copyright laws?*

A. It depends on how old the song is. If it is, say, more than a hundred years old, there should be no problem. It if it still covered by copyright law, whilst it is unlikely a song company would bother about a single line being reproduced in a work of fiction, you should ask for permission first.

Q. *I want to quote from a work of fiction written by someone who died eighty years ago. Can I do so without permission?*

A. Yes, if you are absolutely sure the author has been dead for that long. You should still make acknowledgement in the text, however.

Q. *I want to write an article which will include a good many facts and specific information which I have obtained from various books and magazines. Will I be breaking any copyright laws if I use these?*

A. There is no copyright in facts. Therefore, so long as you use the *facts* only and do not use the words and phrases in the publications you have studied, you will not be infringing the law of copyright.

Q. *I would like to quote from a book, the author of which has been dead for well over a hundred years. However, the author was not English and his work was translated into the English language. Is that work out of copyright and, therefore, available for anyone to use?*

A. You would need to check this with the publishers of the English translation before reproducing any of the book. It is likely that they would hold the copyright of the translation and you would be infringing the law by quoting from it without permission.

Q. *I'm compiling an anthology of various pieces of writing. Must I obtain permission to use them from every writer concerned?*

A. Yes. Permission must be obtained before any material, however short, can be included in an anthology.

Q. *Over several years, I've been collecting humorous extracts from letters, not written by me, which have appeared in print in various publications. I'd like to put them together in an anthology but would I be breaking the law of copyright if I did so?*

A. Yes, you would. The only way round this is to rewrite totally, if the material was anecdotal and the incidents could have happened to anyone.

Q. *I want to use extracts from other writers' work in my own book. Can I do so without obtaining permission?*

A. It depends on the length of the extracts used and the purpose for which they are being included. What is known as the 'fair dealing' clause in the Copyright Act allows for the inclusion of short extracts 'for purposes of criticism and review'. A rough guide is generally considered to be less than 400 words in a single extract but err on the side of caution and always acknowledge the author and, if possible, the publisher.

Libel

Q. *Is there any copyright law which forbids using brand names in a work of fiction? For instance, can I refer to a Mercedes car, a Forte hotel, Coca Cola, etc., without incurring problems?*

A. You are free to use any brand name in your fiction. The danger, here, would lie in *how* you referred to it. If you were to say anything which could be construed as derogatory, you would lay yourself open to a libel action. For example, suppose one of your characters remarked that his (named) car was always breaking down and your novel became a bestseller, the car manufacturer could if it wished sue you for bringing its product into disrepute. In that case, it would be safer to use a fictitious brand name.

Retaining Copyright

Q. *Does a disclaimer at the front of a novel, stating that none of the characters bears any relation to any living person, and so on, free the author from the possible threat of a libel action?*

A.   It would obviously help to reduce such a threat, in the event that someone believed they had been libelled, but only if that statement were true. It would be no defence in law if it were not. It pays to check, so far as is possible, that none of your characters could possibly be identified with any living person. For example, if a character is a doctor with an unusual name specialising in a particular branch of medicine, it would be wise to make sure no such doctor exists.

Q.   *If I were to sell all rights to a story and it was subsequently made into a film, would I be entitled to any of the profits?*

A.   No. Once you part with your copyright, you lose all interest in it.

Q.   *My short story was accepted, and paid for, by a magazine which went out of business before the story was published. Am I now free to try and sell it elsewhere?*

A.   Provided you retained your copyright, then the story belongs to you. You should explain the circumstances in a covering letter when submitting it elsewhere. Editors appreciate honesty from their contributors in case of difficulties arising in the future.

Q.   *I've been writing a regular column for a magazine for almost a year and now I've had an idea for turning these pieces into a book. Does the copyright belong to me or can the magazine claim they own them?*

A.   That depends upon your contract. If you are a direct employee, that is, a member of staff, in all probability, the pieces written for the column belong to the magazine in question. However, if you have been employed on a freelance basis (and have no actual contract), you would have a good case for arguing they belong to you. To avoid any possible dispute, reword them so they are substantially different in form.

Legal Rights

Q. *A magazine printed, without permission, a substantial part of an article of mine which had previously appeared in a specialist publication. I've written to the editor twice but received no reply. I cannot afford to consult a lawyer and wonder if there is any other channel I can use to get redress?*

A. If you belong to a writers' society of any kind, ask them to handle the matter for you (see Useful Addresses, pp. 195–197).

Q. *When an article of mine appeared in print, recently, considerable editorial changes had been made to it so that I hardly recognised it as mine. Does the fact that the magazine rewrote so much of it take away my legal right to the copyright?*

A. The laws of copyright protect *your* words only. If you wish to try to resell your piece, you must offer the original article and not the edited, subsequently published version.

Translations

Q. *I've come across an interesting foreign-language book which isn't available in English. Can I translate it and offer it for publication in the UK without the author's permission?*

A. No. The likelihood is that this book was written by a national of a member of the Universal Copyright Convention and, as such, would be protected by the laws of copyright. Write to the publishers, saying you are interested in translating the book with the intention of offering it to a UK publisher. If they agree, you would be wise to find a publisher for it before you start on the arduous task of translation.

Unpublished Works

Q. *What is the position regarding copyright of unpublished works?*

A. If the author died before 1 August 1989 and the work was unpublished, it will be protected for a further fifty years from that date. If the author died after 1 August 1989, it is protected by current copyright law. If the work was first published posthumously before 1 August 1989 and is in copyright by 1 July 1995, it will be protected for seventy years after publication.

Q. *What is the law as regards letters?*

A. The actual *words* of a letter are protected by copyright law in the same way as any other written material. The paper on which it is written, however, belongs to its recipient. The same applies to diaries and journals. Whoever inherited the deceased's property owns the volumes themselves, but the words written in them are subject to the laws of copyright.

New Copyright Laws

Q. *What is the position after 1 July 1995 regarding works which were considered out of copyright during the previous twenty years?*

A. This is a complex and uncertain area which is still being considered by all official bodies concerned, following the EC Directive.

Moral Rights

Q. *What is meant by the phrase sometimes seen at the front of a book that the author asserts his/her moral rights?*

A. There are three such 'moral rights' conferred by the Copyright Act of 1988. One is the right of the author to be credited whenever the work is published, performed or broadcast. Another gives the author the right to object to any derogatory treatment of the work. The third is the right not to have other work falsely attributed to him/her.

Illustrations

Q. *I've recently purchased a second-hand copy of an old book (published more than seventy years ago by a now defunct publisher) which contains some illustrations I would like to use to accompany an article I'm writing. Is it safe for me to use them?*

A. It would be unwise to do so without first checking on the copyright (which is the same for illustrations as for text). That may be difficult and the chances are that they will be out of copyright. If you decide to risk it, ensure you make due acknowledgement and add a statement to the effect that you have made every effort to trace the holder of the copyright.

Q. *I've been offered a lump sum payment in return for signing over all rights to my book. Would it be unwise to accept?*

A. The standard advice is that authors should rarely agree to part with their copyright. Should you do so and your book later became a bestseller, perhaps being translated into several foreign languages, if you had signed a contract stating that you accepted the stated sum of £X in return for all rights, including your copyright to the work, that would be the end of it. You would not be eligible for any more monies.

Q. *Is there any copyright in plot? I want to use for my own novel the bones of one from a story I've just read.*

A. It would depend upon how closely your storyline, the

incidents and characters involved in it, followed that of an already published novel. Copyright protection extends to the words and form in which ideas are expressed but not to the ideas themselves. If it could be clearly seen, and thus proved, that you had virtually copied another author's story, that would be plagiarism and you could lay yourself open to legal action under the law of copyright.

From time to time, lawsuits have been brought by one author, claiming that the using of the tone, style and characters of his novel amounted to the stealing of his original skill and labour by another author. Stephen Spender blocked publication of a novel, *While England Sleeps*, claiming it drew its plot from his autobiography. Some years ago, another well-known novelist started a lawsuit against the author of a romantic novel, claiming that the plot had been taken from his book. That particular legal action was dropped, however, after it was shown that both his and the other author's story had been based on the plot of a much earlier work well out of copyright.

It is easy to see, therefore, that proving the plot invented by one writer has been stolen by another is extremely difficult. But it is always wise to avoid such possible disputes by coming up with an entirely new plot-line, or at least ensuring you draw on one by an author who has been dead for more than seventy years.

Q. *After an author's death, when the copyright of his works becomes the property of his heirs, can they then legally do what they want with them? For instance, could they try to republish them, if they wished?*

A. It would depend what that author stated in his will. If he did not want what he had written to appear in print, either again or for the first time, he could state in his will that that is his express wish. That, in itself, would not be legally binding on the part of his heirs but he could add certain stipulations. For instance, he could state that, unless his heirs gave a legal undertaking to abide by his wishes, they would not inherit such monies and property they otherwise would. If an author feels strongly about this, he should consult a lawyer when drawing up his will.

Q. *I want to include some old illustrations, photographs and cartoons in a book I'm writing. Do the laws of copyright apply to them, also?*

A. Yes. Such works belong to their creator for seventy years after the creator's death.

Q. *Is there any way to avoid having to obtain permission to quote from other authors' works in my book?*

A. The simplest way is not to quote the exact words and phrases but to paraphrase, that is, express the meaning in your own words.

Pen-Names

Q. *I usually use a pen-name when writing magazine stories. Is their copyright still mine, even though they don't appear under my real name?*

A. The short answer is 'Yes'.

Sequels

Q. *There is, currently, a vogue for sequels to famous novels such as Daphne du Maurier's* Rebecca *and Margaret Mitchell's* Gone With The Wind. *But, surely, the characters in those books are protected by copyright laws and no other writer can virtually steal them to put into another story?*

A. There is, in law, no copyright protection of the actual characters in a story. However, the author (or estate) of the original novel might be able to claim that the second author was trying to profit from the first's good-will and good name. There might, perhaps, be a claim that the original author had suffered damage to his/her reputation should the sequel be considered poorly written.

As with many other aspects of copyright protection, this is a grey area. Therefore, it would be wise for any author considering writing a sequel to a famous story (even if its author is no longer living) to obtain permission from the publisher and/or estate of the original novel before embarking upon the project. They should certainly either obtain legal advice on their publishing contract before signing it or consult the Society of Authors.

So far as US copyright laws are concerned, these often differ from those in the UK and can be more restrictive.

THE BUSINESS SIDE OF WRITING

Q. *If I use a pen-name, would that cause problems over payment? For instance, would my bank accept a cheque made out to a pen-name?*

A. Provided you have informed them of the situation, there should be no problem but they will need proof of your identity and pen-name.

Monies Owed

Q. *A magazine which accepted and printed my short story has since folded and I still haven't been paid for it. What should I do?*

A. In effect, you are a creditor, but in reality it is probable there will be no monies available to pay you. The time spent chasing a relatively small sum is unlikely to be cost-effective and the wisest course may be to put it down to experience and concentrate your efforts into writing something else.

Q. *The magazine which accepted and published my article more than six months ago has not paid me and ignores all letters and invoices. What can I do to get the money owed me?*

A. Try one more letter, sending it by Recorded Delivery so that you have proof of posting. Inform the editor that, if you do not receive payment within one calendar month, you will pursue the matter through the Small Claims Court. Such a threat frequently brings a cheque by return. If it does not, however, be prepared to follow through as it is a relatively easy process. Apply to the Small Claims Court at the county court for the necessary forms. Up to a maximum of £600 claimed, the cost to you will be ten per cent of the sum claimed or a minimum of £10.

Permissions

Q. *I have included some extracts of other authors' work in my book and my contract says I am responsible for obtaining any necessary permissions. Will I have to pay for these myself?*

A. Unless you can persuade your publisher to bear this cost despite what it says in your contract, you will have to do so if payment is requested. However, if the extracts are short enough to come within what is known as the 'fair dealing' clause (see Copyright, p. 181), provided due acknowledgement is made to the author and publisher no payment should be necessary.

Q. *How do I obtain permission to use extracts from another author's work in my book?*

A. You should write to the Permissions Department of the publisher, quoting the extract you want to use, say where it is to appear and ask for permission. It may be that the publisher does not hold the relevant rights; but if they do not they will tell you who does.

Syndication

Q. *What is syndication and how do I go about syndicating my work?*

A. Syndication is selling the same piece (almost invariably non-fiction) to more than one market, either through a syndication firm or by yourself. Payment will be lower than selling First British Serial Rights only and it may not be worth the bother unless you are able to sell to several markets simultaneously. If you decide to try this, you could write to a number of regional newspapers throughout the country, send them examples of your work and offer them a regular column or regular features on specific subjects on which you are some kind of authority or can write easily and well. These topics need to be relevant to readers in whatever part of the country they live. For instance, they might include gardening, car maintenance, DIY, country living, keeping pets or even humorous observations.

Collaboration

Q. *I'm considering collaborating with another writer. What are the implications of this?*

A. The important thing, initially, is to agree on the various aspects involved such as how the work, expenses and any resulting monies will be divided. This should all be clearly set out in a legally binding contract signed by both of you.

Q. *I've been asked to ghost-write someone's life story but I don't know how much to charge or if I should ask for a split in royalties if the book is successful. Can you offer any advice?*

A. If the book is to be self-published, it is up to you to work out, as near as possible, how long it will take you to listen to the story and then write it up and charge accordingly. If you hope to interest a bona fide publisher in it, it would be normal to expect fifty per cent of any advance and subsequent royalties. But before starting work on such a book make sure you have a legally binding contract.

Extra Sales

Q. *I've just learned that a book club has offered to buy copies of my first book but I wonder if that will be a good thing for me?*

A. Book clubs operate by purchasing substantial quantities of books at a heavily discounted price from the publisher. The books are then sold to the public, usually by mail order, more cheaply than they are available in bookshops. Although the royalties an author receives from these sales are low, this can be compensated for by the volume of sales. It also provides considerable exposure in publicising both author and book and so, generally, it is to be welcomed.

Grants

Q. *Is it possible to obtain a government grant of any kind when starting out to become a writer?*

A. Almost certainly not. The old Government Enterprise Scheme Allowance, which did cover writers, has been changed to the Business Support Grant. Contact your nearest local authority Enterprise Agency for Small

Business Training and Advice and enquire but writers are currently not eligible for a grant.

Income Tax

Q. *If I can find a literary agent, will his fees be tax-deductible?*

A. Yes. This is a legitimate expense which can be set against income tax.

Q. *If I attend a writers' conference, can I offset this against income tax?*

A. Once you are actually making money from your writing, all such expenses are tax-deductible. Similarly, books, stationery, equipment, postage and a proportion of telephone bills, heating and lighting in your home, if you use part of it for your writing, can all be set against income tax.

Q. *If I buy a word processor or any other equipment such as a fax machine, can I offset these against tax?*

A. Yes. There are capital allowances for any necessary equipment purchased, but these allowances are spread over several years.

Q. *If I employ an accountant, can I charge his fees against tax?*

A. Yes.

Q. *I intend using a room in my home as an office for my writing activities. Can I claim tax relief for this use?*

A. You can, but you should seek advice before doing so to ensure you do not become liable for Capital Gains Tax should you sell your home in the future.

SUMMING UP

Finally, your last few questions have been answered and the loose ends tied up. You are confident you know how to work alongside an editor or others involved in publishing your writing. You understand something of the laws of copyright and how to handle the business side of writing. You can now make a decision as to whether it would advantageous to join one of the many societies open to you and have looked at the pros and cons of paying to see your work in print and perhaps at entering literary competitions.

Your feet are now firmly set on the path of success and you can move forward with confidence, knowing you have ahead of you a lifelong interest which can also provide you with an income, whether it be large or small. The rest is up to you, to your own determination and perseverance. I wish you every success.

Appendix

COMPETITIONS, AWARDS AND PRIZES

Numerous competitions are run both nationally and locally. Some are organised by writers' groups, others by national magazines, newspapers, large commercial companies and, from time to time, by the BBC. Details of the following appear in the national press, relevant magazines and writing magazines:

The Ian St James Award (short story)
Swanage Arts Festival Literary Competition (short story and poetry)
Bridport Arts Centre (short story and poetry)
Dillington Short Story Competition
Peterloo Poets Poetry Competition
Envoi Magazine International Poetry Competition
Stand Magazine International Short Story Competition
The *European/Raconteur* (short story)
The *Guardian*–Stop Press Travel Writing Competition
The Arvon Poetry Competition (in association with the *Observer*)
The Dennis Potter Television Play of the Year Award, a new annual award set up in memory of Dennis Potter, run by the BBC's Television Drama Department. Entrants must be

sponsored by a production company.

The Kathleen Fidler Award for an unpublished novel for children aged eight to twelve (run by The Book Trust)

The McKitterick Prize for a novel by writers over forty (run by the Society of Authors)

The Betty Trask Award for a first novel by writers under thirty-five (run by the Society of Authors)

The Catherine Cookson Fiction Prize for an unpublished novel (run by Transworld Publishers Ltd, 61/63 Uxbridge Road, London W5 5SA)

USEFUL ADDRESSES

Association of Little Presses
30 Greenhill
Hampstead High Street
London NW3 5UA
Tel: 0171–435 1889

The Book Trust
Book House
45 East Hill
London SW18 2QZ

Crime Writers' Association
PO Box 172
Tring
Herts HP23 5LP

International PEN
9/10 Charterhouse Buildings
Goswell Road
London EC1M 7AT

The London Library
14 St James's Square
London SW1Y 4LG

The National Council for the Training of Journalists
Carlton House
Hemnal Street
Epping
Essex CM16 4NL

New Playwrights Trust
Interchange Studios
Dalby Street
London NW5 3NQ

The Poetry Society
22 Betterton Street
London WC2H 9BU

The Public Lending Right Office
Bayheath House
Prince Regent Street
Stockton-on-Tees
Cleveland TS18 1DF

The Romantic Novelists' Association
Hon. Secretary, Hilary Johnson
5 St Agnes Gate
Wendover
Bucks HP22 6DP

The Society of Authors
84 Drayton Gardens
London SW10 9SB

The Society of Women Writers & Journalists
Hon. Secretary, Jean Hawkes
110 Whitehall Road
Chingford
London E4 6DW

Teddington Arts Performance Showcase (TAPS)
Jill James
Broom Road
Teddington TW11 9NT
Tel: 0181–977 3252

The Writers Advice Centre
6 Bramble Way
Send Marsh
Woking
Surrey GU23 6LL
Tel: 01483–223860

The Writers' Guild of Great Britain
430 Edgware Road
London W2 1EH

WRITING CONFERENCES AND SEMINARS

The Arvon Foundation
Totleigh Barton
Sheepwash
Devon EX21 5NS
(Also at Lumb Bank, Heptonstall, Hebden Bridge, West
Yorkshire HX7 6DF; and Moniack Mhor, Teavarran, Kiltarlity,
Beauly, Inverness-shire IV4 7HT)

Dillington House (writing courses)
Ilminster
Somerset TA19 9DT
Tel: 01460–52427

Southampton Writers' Conference (annually, April, at the
    University)
Organiser, Barbara Large
University of Southampton Adult Continuing Education

Department
Highfield
Southampton SO9 5NH
Tel: 01703–593469

Writers' Holiday (annually, July, South Wales)
Administrator, Anne Hobbs
30 Pant Road
Newport
Gwent NP9 5PR

The Writers' Summer School (annually, mid-August, at The
   Hayes Conference Centre, Swanwick, Derbyshire)
Hon. Secretary, Brenda Courtie
The New Vicarage
Parsons Street
Woodford Halse
Daventry
Northants NN11 3RE

Writing holidays in France with Nancy Smith
Adam Cottage
St Mary's Street
Axbridge
Somerset BS26 2BN

USEFUL PUBLICATIONS

Magazines

Acclaim, The New Writers Club Ltd, PO Box 101, Tunbridge
   Wells, Kent TN4 8YD
Fiction Writers' Monthly, 163 Joralemon Street, Brooklyn
   Heights, NY 11201, USA
Freelance Market News, Freelance Press Services, Cumberland
   House, Lissadel Street, Manchester M6 6GG

Freelance Writing & Photography, Clarendon Court, Over Wallop, Stockbridge, Hants SO20 8HU

Quartos Magazine, BCM–Writer, London WC1N 3XX

Romantic Times, 163 Joralemon Street, Brooklyn Heights, NY 11210, USA

The Writer, 120 Boylston Street, Boston, MA 02116, USA (available from Freelance Press Services)

Writer's Digest, 9933 Alliance Road, Cincinnati, OH 45242, USA (available from Freelance Press Services, p. 198)

Writers' Monthly, 18/20 High Road, London N22 6DN

Writers News, PO Box 4, Nairn, Highland IV12 4HU

Writing Magazine, PO Box 4, Nairn, Highland IV12 4HU (available from some newsagents)

Books

The Art of Dramatic Writing, by Lajos Egri (Simon & Schuster)

Becoming a Playwright, by David Campton (Robert Hale)

Directory of Writers' Circles, compiled by Jill Dick (available from Oldacre, Hordens Park Road, Chapel en le Frith, Derbyshire SK12 6SY)

The Fiction Writers' Handbook, by Nancy Smith (Piatkus)

Fowler's Dictionary of Modern English (Oxford University Press)

Guide to Literary Prizes, Grants and Awards in Britain and Ireland (available from The Book Trust)

How to Make Money from Freelance Writing, by Andrew Crofts (Piatkus)

How to Write for Children, by Marion Hough (Writers News)

Interviewing for Journalists, by Joan Clayton (Piatkus)

Journalism for Beginners, by Joan Clayton (Piatkus)

The Methuen Dictionary of Clichés, by Christine Ammer (Methuen)

The Novelist's Guide, by Margret Geraghty (Piatkus)

The Oxford Dictionary for Writers and Editors (Oxford University Press)

The Oxford Guide to English Usage (Oxford University Press)

Research for Writers, by Ann Hoffman (A. & C. Black)

Roget's Thesaurus (Penguin)

Successful Article Writing, by Gillian Thornton (Writers News)

The Thirty-Six Dramatic Situations, by Georges Polti (The Writer Inc.; available from Freelance Press Services)

1000 Markets for Freelance Writers, by Robert Palmer (Piatkus)

Time to Learn, National Institute of Adult Continuing Education, 21 De Montfort Street, Leicester LE1 7GE; tel: 0116–255 1451

Twenty Master Plots, by Ronald B. Tobias (Piatkus)

Writers' and Artists' Year Book (A. & C. Black, annual)

The Writer's Handbook (PEN/Macmillan, annual)

Writing Historical Fiction, by Rhona Martin (A. & C. Black)

Writing the Modern Mystery, by Barbara Norville (Writer's Digest Books)

Writing Poetry, by Doris Corti (Writers News)

Writing Proposals and Synopses that Sell, by André Jute (Writers News)

Writing Your Life Story, by Nancy Smith (Piatkus)

THE WRITERS ADVICE CENTRE
(headed by Nancy Smith)

Offers an honest, objective and in-depth critique of your Novel/Short Story/ Autobiography

Publishers and editors have little time to say *why* they reject a manuscript. The Writers Advice Centre can provide this missing information. They also offer Personal Introductions to Publishers/ Editors where appropriate

For details, send SAE to:
The Writers Advice Centre,
6 Bramble Way,
Send Marsh,
Woking,
Surrey GU23 6LL